Bits of Heaven

AMY LYNN

Bits of Heaven
by Amy Lynn

 Unless otherwise identified, Scripture quotations are from the King James Version of the Bible.

ISBN 1-58169-029-0
For Worldwide Distribution
Printed in the U.S.A.

Evergreen Press
An Imprint of Genesis Communications, Inc.
P.O. Box 91011 • Mobile, AL 36691
(334) 665-0022 • 800-367-8203
Email: GenesisCom@aol.com

Table of Contents

* Denotes Poetry

Preface

If we look closely, there are bits of heaven all around us...in the eyes of our children, in the hearts of our friends, even in the smile of strangers. Life holds many lessons that sometimes go unnoticed. We must see through the eyes of faith and recognize the divinity in all events big and small. God's miracles never cease. Life is composed of endless decisions and choices, and each one can bring us a bit closer to heaven.

Nature especially holds many small miracles, tiny treasures patiently waiting to be uncovered. We can abundantly learn the blessings of gratitude by observing its characteristic simplicity. A portion of God's power is unveiled in the many precious circular patterns that are revolving in brilliant symmetry in nature.

We can see bits of heaven when we turn to our hearts also. We are all born to follow God's path, to experience His destiny, and to discover all that we are in His eyes. The lessons we learn along our journey and the miracles and gifts we cherish along the way become the perfect guide to lead us to the end of our journey. On the other side of what we see lies the eternal beauty of all that we have been created to be.

The following pages contain short stories and poems, each one written with the intention of warming the heart and stirring the soul. Many of them are based upon my own experiences or those of others that I have encountered along the way. Some of the details have been altered to add variety and protect anonymity.

This book will especially benefit women who struggle with the issues of motherhood, single-parenting, marriage, divorce, and recovery. My hope is that each reader can identify with at least one of the characters, perhaps recognizing their own journey. We are all sojourners in faith; we travel to the same end. Each of us with our unique gifts and talents, all follow One who has written our destiny in eternity.

Amy Lynn, 1999

Dedication

To my dear mother Mary Jo,
who continues to show me the ways
of faith.

Also a special thanks to my family and friends
who inspired many of these stories.

There Once Was a Woman

There once was a woman who walked by our house twice every day. Through the varying seasons and harsh elements she trotted, step after step, from wherever her home was to wherever her destination was to be. In the summer, she dressed in a light, flower print smock which was soaked in tiny beads of sweat that dripped from her bony shoulders. In the winter, she covered her smock with a heavy wool coat. Woven in dark threaded gray, its hood surrounded her face in an assembly of tan fur. All that poked out was the tip of her slim nose.

She stepped her way back and forth day after day, through seasons of change. Her steps added special meaning to the quiet rhythm of her life. She never seemed rushed, even in temperatures well below zero. She simply fastened a crocheted scarf around her nose and dipped her head to escape the bite of the winter wind.

When spring finally blossomed, she shed her heavy cloak and scarf to reveal her gray, stringy hair, which rustled in the brisk strokes of the fresh breeze. She paused near the pink and white budding trees along her path as if to absorb their aroma. The springtime wind seemed to fill her spirit; God's creation filled her soul. She was remarkably beautiful in a simplistic way. She had a glow of certainty about her. She highlighted the trail with sparkles of eternity.

We assumed this unusual, yet intriguingly unique woman must be very poor, for why else would she walk to and fro, day after day? We pitied her circumstance and offered her rides whenever we saw her jaunting by, yet each time she refused, insisting she found great enjoyment along her trail. She always smiled in a grand gratitude that sparkled in a dance of enjoyment about her face. Although we did not understand her refusal, we respected her contentment and continued along our merry way.

One day, we noticed she did not walk by our house, either by sunrise or sunset. We thought that perhaps she may be ill. We hoped she had not been injured or hurt along her mysterious path. The memory of her predictable appearance taunted us for the next several days. We watched the sidewalks she normally trotted, yet they remained empty from her presence.

It came as a surprise one afternoon when we caught a glimpse of the woman in an old, black car. She was driving very slowly, as if she were tracing her footsteps along the sidewalk beside the road, remembering the tiny treasures she discovered along the path she had walked each day. Her eyes peeked over the steering wheel and traveled in horizontal exploration of everything she used to pause to enjoy. Her gray, stringy hair dangled out the half open window so as to capture a taste of the creation she once absorbed completely.

We were relieved to see she had survived the icy winter and tickled to find she now could drive her way to and fro. We soon grew accustomed to the routine passing of her car and before long, forgot altogether her strangely unique journey on foot. Her once-a-day visit by our house faded into the brilliant colored leaves of autumn.

Then, one beautiful October day, as the dark orange and bright yellow leaves danced against a navy blue sky, we saw her. She was walking again from wherever her home was to wherever her destination was to be. Her gray hair twisted circles around her sparkling face that harbored a smile as bright as the moon. Peace seemed to walk beside her silhouette of serenity. She glided with each step as if her spirit were being lifted in the wind.

We noticed over the next several days that she continued to walk to and fro, no longer using her car at all. Even as the hands of time turned the season back to bitter cold, she walked, never hurried, never rushed. We thought that perhaps she was having car problems and offered again to give her a ride to wherever her destination was, but again she politely refused.

"I would rather walk," she assured us as she confidently gazed through the fogged glass of our car window.

The following summer, we were walking home from a nearby park when we met this curious woman just as she was arriving at her home. We were surprised to see it was quite nice, at least not as we had pictured it. We watched her walk past her car, which was still parked in her driveway, and up the stairs leading to her front door.

We had to run ahead and stop her. We could not contain our inquisitive minds any longer. As she walked up her stairs, we greeted her with a simple smile and hello. She stopped and turned to face us with a friendly warmth that immediately comforted our uneasiness.

"We notice you are out walking every day again," we said as she paused on the stoop of her front door.

"Yes," she replied with a smile.

"Are you having car trouble?" we asked glancing at the old black car in her driveway.

"No," she responded with a giggle.

"Then why do you always walk to and fro, especially in the bitter cold winter?" we asked, no longer able to disguise our curiosity.

In an uncompromisingly friendly tone of voice, she explained, "I tried to drive, but I missed so very much!"

We had to inquire further, as it appeared she found hidden treasures along her path, treasures unseen and unappreciated by most.

"What types of things did you miss?" we asked, eagerly awaiting the unveiling of her secrets.

"I missed the pastel etching that marks the rise of the sun, the illumination of the tree branches sketched across the dawning sky, and the chirping lullabies of birds as they build their nests. I missed the fragrant perfume that pours from the cup of a blossoming flower and the freedom of spirit found in the breeze. I missed the sun as it rests upon a horizon swirled in apricot and plum, and the mystic glow of the moon as it covers the earth to rest." She said all this as if she was a true friend of nature, a special child of God.

We thanked her for sharing her inspiration with us and continued our journey toward home. We slowed our quick steps to match the familiar glide she had eloquently displayed so many times in passing by our house. The wind twisted through our hair as it rustled through a field of dandelions alongside our path. We began to feel the warm glow that surrounded the spirit of the woman. The slower we walked, the deeper we were absorbed in God's creation as it stroked our hearts and soothed our minds.

As the years turned the remaining pages of our lives, we no longer wondered what the old woman found along the trail from wherever her home was to wherever her destination was to be. We came to understand that her home was born in the freedom she found within her soul, and her destination remained with her wherever she was. She had found a bit of heaven!

God's Miracles Sown in Nature

Nature's freshness captivates the soul; it lightens the spirit with an inner essence that's whole.

Nature's melody of songs brings peace to the drift; synchronization like magic strokes the heart with this gift.

Painted rainbows, rustic sunsets, in skies dressed in dark; twisted trees, scattered flowers, a musk meadow lark.

Nature's tender embrace brings hope with each breath, reviving weak and weary, within peaceful inner depth.

Rolling wheat fields of gold, planted seeds sown in love; mystic raindrops bring life, released from above.

Nature's innocence is pure; her circular patterns run free. Her reflections bring closer heaven's destiny.

The hands of time gently rock as each day unfolds. Nature's moments in planned unison are ours to behold.

A Dainty Bouquet of Pink Flowers

"What an exhausting week!" I thought as I surrendered two minutes of my day to melt back in the sage lounge chair in our family room. It was Wednesday—just mid-week—and I was already exhausted from commitments. My mom always called me an "overachiever," and today I believed her.

During the moment of relaxation, my mind reflected on the many changes in my life since the year began. Just a year ago, I was promoted in my business career to a top executive position. I also began therapy for emotional struggles at the same time. I grew up in an abusive home and the psychological implications of this, along with my own struggles to recover from depression, were beginning to wear me down.

I still found it hard to believe that this year brought me such a change in heart. I turned thirty just prior to the turn of the new year; and with my birthday, I made a decision to finally begin taking care of myself. Through hard work in counseling, the help of family and friends, and regular prayer, I finally realized that I had spent my whole life doing what I thought I was *supposed* to do, not what I really *wanted* to do.

With the help of God, I resigned my ten-year career with a large international firm. I would love to say I gave this position up in complete willingness, but my conscience reminds me of the struggles I had over that decision, which still remain at times.

Ever since childhood, the Lord has been my Shepherd. I always had a deep desire to serve Him, yet spent each of my days running my own show.

Even though I believed and even loved God, I had never been willing—prior to this year—to let Him direct my life completely. With my decision at the beginning of the year to take care of myself, I searched my heart and found my dreams. In the hand of God, I made a commitment to pursue my calling.

Tonight I would teach a Bible study for first, second, and third graders. *I really should be reviewing my lesson plans*, I thought as I stretched my body out on the lounger. I had spent the day gardening, something I have always enjoyed. I resigned to become a full-time mom this year, a rewarding commitment I had always dreamed of. With any dream comes sacrifice, and time for myself was no longer as abundant.

Even though I no longer worked outside of the home, I usually finished the day in the same exhaustion I was all too familiar with. At least now my incredible need to overachieve was working to build God's kingdom, rather than that of my own little world. Although the grief of giving up a wonderful career tweaked my emotions at times, my faith in God's plans was enough to relieve my anxiety.

I really had to wonder what God willed on that particular night, however. When I am worn out, it becomes difficult to see the gifts He places before me. "Doing my best, despite my doubt" was thankfully becoming a habit, so I pulled myself up and went into the kitchen, where my untouched lesson plans awaited me on the table. After settling myself in the chair, I opened the book and began to read the outline.

This evening, I was to teach the children about some of the virtues of being a good Christian. The book suggested focusing on truth, honesty, justness, good will, and good rapport as important qualities. At the end of the session, I was to lead an inner group discussion and conclude by asking the children if they knew that Jesus was in their heart. The lesson called me to announce that any child who had not yet asked Jesus to come into their heart could stay after class, and I would help them enter into a personal relationship with Him.

In my tired and limited vision, I pondered the fact that these kids were too young to make such a commitment in faith. Even if they were ready, I questioned my own ability to perform such an incredible task; after all, I am not a minister. Almost immediately, I felt a warm confidence surround my heart as God whispered through my soul, "Don't worry. I will not ask you to do anything you cannot do." Again, I made a decision to "simply do my best, despite my doubt." I finished my review of the plans, closed the book, and fixed dinner for my kids, after which we headed for the church.

We kicked off Bible study by singing the "Whirlybirds Anthem." Next, two other teachers and I sat in a circle with the children on a colored carpet, where I read the Bible story and talked about some of the virtues outlined in the lesson plans. After explaining that Jesus possesses all of these virtues, I insecurely announced that anyone who had not asked Jesus into their heart and wanted to make this special commitment tonight, could stay in the room after class.

With that, I turned the class over to the teachers in charge of activity time. I had no expectation that any children would take advantage of my offer; after all, they were so young. I spent the rest of the evening helping the children cut, glue, and create cards and greetings for the new pastor at our church. The room quickly became a mess, and I found my fingers glued together, and pieces of streamers hanging from my hair.

Eight o'clock soon approached, and an assistant teacher announced it was time for everyone to clean up his or her work space and line up to sing in the sanctuary. I scrambled to help the other teachers restore the room to a respectable condition. As the children began exiting rapidly, one child remained. Her name was Andrea. I had felt a special bond with this child all year. It was not unlike Andrea to linger around after class.

An assistant teacher glanced at Andrea and warned her in a helpful voice that she would be late to the sanctuary. "You had best hurry, Andrea. You will be late for the closing song."

Andrea just stood there, and I remember thinking, *Come on, Andrea, please listen to directions.* When Andrea did not budge, the other teacher more insistently requested that she join the rest of the children. Andrea's big brown eyes searched the room for me as she meekly said, "But, she said I could stay after class if I wanted."

Suddenly it dawned on me that Andrea was not standing there to simply lollygag. Andrea was ready to ask Jesus to come into her heart, and she was looking directly at me. God lifted my spirit that evening as I took her by the tiny hand and led her to a private place by a window where we both sat down. With legs crossed, we faced each other as I told her how honored I felt that she asked me to help her seek this special connection.

At first, I felt an insecure awkwardness as I realized I had no idea how to do this. Following the whispers of my heart, I asked Andrea to place her hand over her heart as I did the same, and I grasped her left hand in mine. As I began to pray with this young child, God guided my words. I could feel the Spirit at work.

When we were done, I said "Amen," and we both opened our eyes to face each other. A warm dampness swelled in my eyes as I saw her brown ones sparkling with tears. She stared at me as if to say she'd entered the beginning of a new life. We slowly stood up together and hand-in-hand began walking toward the sanctuary.

Andrea stopped me before we reached the door. She picked up a dainty bouquet of pink flowers and handed it to me. "Here," she said. "I picked these for you before class. They're from my yard."

When we arrived, the music was ending. I thanked Andrea for the beautiful flowers and said goodbye. Before leaving the sanctuary, I had to pause in gratitude. As I looked from the cross in front of the church, down to the dainty bouquet of pink flowers folded in my hands, I realized that God could help me do anything, even welcome another child into His kingdom. I was reminded again that special night that God's gifts often come in small packages.

Since I resigned my position in my former business, I have been blessed with many gifts of the kingdom of God. I have learned that although I do not always know where I am going, I can be willing to follow in faith. God does not ask me to do anything beyond those talents He planted within my soul long ago. My decision to follow my dreams has placed me on a path of peace and happiness in His eternal grace. I can build children in faith, which perhaps is the most rewarding job anyone can have.

Tiny Treasures

The bluebird beckoned me awake to start a busy day. His echoed call of yonder dreams reminded me to pray.

I know this may sound silly—without God my day is lost. So I must pray each morning, to follow despite the cost.

Each day holds tiny treasures when I follow in God's will; each moment special meaning. My life is such a thrill.

The sunrise turns another page to reveal my guided script. When I follow God's inscriptions, within His love I sit.

Tiny treasures are mine to give, as I enjoy as well
They enrich my soul so very much; the hands of time will tell.

And so I lay my golden hair on the pillow where I slumber. The sunset kisses my day goodbye as I rest in comfort under…

Scattered stars of answered prayers and dreams that have come true. Thank God for tiny treasures; my life alone won't do.

A Dream to Become

Amber gazed through the car window, smudged in the breath of her excitement, as she sat in the back seat anticipating her arrival in Kansas City, MO, where the weekend ahead may hand her the answer to her dreams. Amber has always dreamed of becoming a superstar model. She was selected just days ago to be presented at a regional Model Search event, which featured several top modeling agents and producers.

Amber convinced her mom, through heartfelt pleading, that she was destined to share her beauty with the world. Her mom, sheltered in a conservative and serious personality, had numerous reservations. Having modeled herself through high school and college, she was not comfortable with the risks this incredible experience might present.

After several days of pleading, her mom finally realized that Amber's dream to become a model mimicked her own childhood desire to become a beautician. In realizing that she was given the opportunity to reach for her dreams by attending beauty school, her mom hesitantly agreed to support Amber's efforts to become a model.

Days of thoughtful evaluation led to that special day when the excitement began. "Amber!" her mom had called from the kitchen. "I have been giving thought to the idea of you becoming a model." Amber's eyes shimmered in hope as she listened to her mother's announcement. "You are one of the most beautiful girls in the world," her mom continued, "not because of your amber green eyes, nor because of your pretty ginger hair. Your beauty is also within and radiates to highlight your physical appearance. If you can remember through this experience that true beauty begins within, then I will support you in your dream."

Amber's mom always seemed to tell her things she already knew. But, she patiently listened with the intention of receiving her mother's blessing and jumped high in the kitchen after listening to her mother's endorsement. Her mom's words sent her on a parade of skips, bounces, and leaps. Her dream to become a model was placed at the beginning of the road to reality. She was given the chance to capture her destiny.

Days later, Amber and her mom visited the elegant hotel, where "Model Search America" was selecting regional models to present at the upcoming convention. As they drove the car into the huge spiral parking garage, Amber looked at her mom from the corner of her eye for reassurance. "It will be the way it is supposed to be," her Mom said as she pulled into a parking stall. "You are beautiful. They will see your true personality shine."

A huge line awaited them as they shuffled their way inside to find a seat. They were told to complete an application, find a place at the end of the line, and wait until Amber's turn came up to interview with the model scout. A dull pain crept in her mother's stomach as she watched hopeful people pass by this handsomely smug man, one by one, showing him their best smile. As they advanced closer to the front of the huge ballroom, Amber looked again at her mother for encouragement. "Don't worry, sweetheart. You're beautiful," her mother whispered.

The moment finally arrived. Amber and her mom moved from the front of the line into the spot of final truth. Amber looked innocently at the scout and said "Hi," in her naturally sweet way, while her mom handed him her application. As he took the piece of paper to lay in the smaller of two piles, the scout smiled and said, "Your daughter has beautiful eyes."

His compliment offered temporary reassurance as Amber and her mom found a seat in the ballroom where they awaited the man to announce the chosen models. After a considerable amount of time passed, a loud voice announced a schedule for the remaining activities. They would be calling several names. "If you hear your name," the scout announced, "it is time to leave. The people remaining will be our chosen models and will be presented in the upcoming "Model Search Convention."

Amber's heart skipped a beat as she realized this was it. The time had come for her to either realize her dream or let it go. Her mom reassured her, "Don't worry, sweetie. They won't call your name. He saw the beauty behind your eyes." Amber relaxed a little as she heard these words of encouragement.

"Scott Smith, Judy Ramsy, Carol Wagner," the scout began rattling names faster than an auctioneer at a flea market. Between each name Amber breathed one more sigh of relief. "Amber…Johnson." Amber's heart stopped, but she quickly regained her composure when she heard the last name was not Zimmerman. Her mother's fingers closed over hers as she again said, "Don't worry, he will not call your name. You are beautiful."

After what seemed like hours of name rattling, the scout announced that he was finished. He reminded everyone who heard his or her name to leave. He assured them that just because he did not select them, they should not give up on their dream. Amber and her mom looked at each other as their eyes danced in excited gratitude. They bounced in their seats as they listened to the congratulations and the instructions for the upcoming convention.

It was nearly ten o'clock before they finished receiving all of the directions and information that concerned the convention in April. Sleep brushed their eyes as they drove home from the hotel. Despite their worn emotions, anticipation filled the air.

April had finally arrived, and Amber found herself sitting in even greater anticipation in the back seat of the car with her brother, as her mom and dad drove her to the convention. Gazing out the sunny window, she spotted a path of clouds shaped like stepping stones. She pictured herself walking on them across the sky on a path that led to stardom. Her hopeful thoughts were interrupted by the voice of her mom excitedly declaring that they had arrived in Kansas City. Amber quickly sat up and searched around the interstate for signs of direction.

Soon, a magnificent skyscraper began to emerge on the horizon. Her mom pointed to it saying, "There it is!" Amber scooted forward to get a better look at the convention hotel. The building was larger than she had even imagined—its upper stories seemed to almost reach the clouds.

"Here we are!" her dad said as he drove up the circular entrance to the gates of the hotel. "Why don't you guys go in and find a seat in the convention? Your brother and I will park the car, unload the luggage, and check in."

Amber and her mom hopped out of the car without hesitation and eagerly walked through the front gates of the hotel. They passed elegant crystal sculptures and fountains as they walked up three flights of marble stairs to the convention ballroom. Amber had a skip in her step as they entered this colossal room decorated in dazzling crystal chandeliers. She and her mom found a seat and began reviewing the program guide for the weekend ahead.

While her mother highlighted various events and read the schedule, Amber's eyes roamed the polished runway, which stretched along the front of the ballroom and crossed the room from one side to the other, extending out in a wide finger toward the center of the stage. "This is where I might realize my dreams," she thought. "This is where I could become a superstar model."

They wait half an hour for the introduction to this fantastic weekend of excitement and learning. Her mom leaned over before it began and with a kiss, she whispered, "No matter what happens, you are beautiful. Just be yourself and have fun."

Amber did not need to hear that she should be herself; but again, her mother needed to tell her what she already knew in her heart. She smiled and grasped her mother's hand as throbbing, upbeat music began to fill the room. Amber covered her ears at first, but slowly removed her hands as she joined the crowd's anticipation. This was finally it! Her dream to become a model was on the verge of happening.

The model scout who selected Amber entered the front stage as the music began to fade, and he outlined the program for the weekend. "Most of the activities and workshops are in preparation for Sunday," he announced. "Sunday will be the day when top modeling agents from around the world will line up right here, along this runway, to watch you walk in front of them. Along with a team of top models, I will work with you throughout the weekend to prepare you for the final runway appearance."

The panel of models was then introduced. Amber recognized some of them from her selection back home. She liked Catherine Mogull, in particular, who suggested that modeling success is dependent on personality. "Just be yourself and enjoy it. The most important thing is not to forget who you are." Of course, Amber's mom also enjoyed these inspiring words that this beautiful young woman shared with her daughter.

The course of the weekend proved to be highly exhaustive and intense.

Amber and her mom broke away whenever they could to enjoy family time with her dad and brother. They usually found them lounging and swimming in the pool or watching movies in the room. Each time Amber excitedly reported what she had just learned and what was yet to come. Her family stepped into her dream and surrounded her with encouragement. She felt their love and support.

Early Sunday morning, Amber and her mom rushed around the hotel room dressing and fixing their hair. Amber selected a simple green dress that matched her eyes. Her mom did not fuss long with her hair, gently brushing it under a few strokes until all the tangles were removed. Amber insisted on just being herself, with limited decoration.

"Are you ready?" her mom asked, gazing at her truly beautiful daughter in the mirror.

"Yes," Amber replied with confidence as she met her mother's gaze with a smile.

"Let's do it!"

They nervously strode down the long corridor, which separated their room from the magnificent ballroom where Amber would walk the runway. Approaching the large double door, Amber's mom once again reminded her that it would be the way it was supposed to be. "No matter the outcome, sweetie, you are beautiful inside and out. Your beauty blossoms from your tender soul, and your inner kindness will highlight your outward beauty."

Some may think her mother reassured Amber in this way because she was not outwardly beautiful. Quite to the contrary, Amber was very pretty. Ever since she was a baby, people would comment on how beautiful she is. The model scout did not select anyone he did not think had a reasonable chance for success at the convention. He did not waste his time or the time of others. Amber's mom reminded her that it was an honor to be selected locally, despite the outcome of this larger event.

But Amber's dream was to become a superstar model. Anything short of selection by a top-modeling agent was bound to disappoint her. Her hopes continued to rise as she and her mother entered the ballroom and found a seat by the long runway. They anxiously waited for the final presentation instruction to begin.

The director entered on stage to announce the lineup for the walk on the runway. He introduced the panel of agents who would view the presentation. Among them were agents from Paris, Milan, New York, Japan, and other key commercial art and modeling locations. He also introduced television advertising producers and leading international talent scouts.

Amber's mom finally began to feel the pressure of the weekend. Her little girl would walk in front of all of these famous, incredibly influential people. Suddenly, she forgot all of the "be yourself" talks she had lectured, and fell captive to this incredible moment. She found herself telling Amber frantically how to smile, who to smile at, how to walk, which direction to face; you name it, she outlined what to do. Amber asked her mother in frustration to let her be. "I will be all right, Mom. Really," she said.

The time finally arrived for Amber to line up. The music began, and her mom felt it pulsate her heart. Her palms became sweaty as she watched the models step onto the runway one at a time for their introduction. Many walked in a predetermined style with smiles pasted on their face; others melted to the music; many walked in sensual insecurity. Her mom became more uncomfortable with each model that glided by.

Her spirit softened to see her daughter step into the light of the runway. It was as if she carried a light of her own. Amber stepped up the stairs with a smiling confidence. Her mother suddenly forgot all of the last minute instructions for Amber's performance. Her smile joined Amber's as her daughter began to walk the runway as though she was stepping into her dreams. Her natural beauty radiated her path. She was indeed born in beauty from the Spirit. Her mom paused in gratitude to thank the Lord. Warm tears began to flow down her mother's face as she finally realized that Amber already had understood all that she had tried to share with her about true beauty. Walking in front of famous people from around the world, Amber did not compromise who she was. She stepped up to the runway as herself—a special child of God—and met the eyes of every agent with a wholesome sparkle. With each step, she revealed a page of her true personality. With each smile, she spread her light.

Amber has a dream to become, not unlike many that dream of fulfilling their destiny. In reaching for her dreams, she remains firmly grounded in her true value. No matter what Amber does, she will never forget those words from her mother that "True beauty begins with who we are." This was not a learning experience for Amber alone; her mother, too, deepened her own understanding of this message by watching the example provided so naturally by her own daughter. Who says parents always know best?

As the years pass, Amber continues to strive toward meeting challenges and goals. Although she was not selected for a modeling contract at the "model search" convention, she went on to discover there are far better ways to share her beauty with others, and even though she may have achieved the dream of being involved in this convention, she declined invitations to future conventions. She even began questioning her ideas of destiny.

Through this experience, Amber learned that we realize certain dreams only to let them go. They are simply meant to bring us closer to who we are created to be; they show us a bit more of our true destiny. And this is what life is all about!

The Angels of Nature

The angels of nature are everywhere, upon the breeze...they sing in the air. They shed their light upon the earth, in sparkles of sunshine they spread rebirth. The angels of nature twist through the trees... they shuffle and muffle and dance with the leaves. As each leaf falls and sways all around, an angel is there to guide it to ground. The angels of nature sound in the sky... with trumpets of clouds they tell stories of why...The world is so hungry and faith seems alone. If we follow God's way, we will all return home. The angels of nature fly in the wind, their freshness and beauty brush against skin... as the tips of their wings stroke the depths of the heart...forever through fate, they show us our part. The angels of nature reflect in the light...their delicate jewels a magnificent sight. And each jewel is treasured beyond our belief, as they dance upon water... they shimmer in peace. The angels of nature sing with the birds. Their songs travel far... love's melody without words. Each note lifts the world in the chorus of God; they whisper His will near and abroad. The angels of nature fall with the rain. In sweet drops of mercy...they wash away pain. And soak through the soul to replenish our hope. Like prisms of light, each drop helps us cope. The angels of nature sail through the meadows. They whisper God's glory stirred in the shadows...of golden stocks in shades dressed with brown, telling tales of eternity... they show us our crown. The angels of nature dance with the flowers. They bring us to joy using God-given powers. Their wings shake the petals and dance in the breeze. They color the wind with beauty and ease. Each angel of nature is like a butterfly. Her wings flutter in freedom...the heart hears her sigh. Her delicate colors bring serenity and peace, her faith, hope, and love...are never to cease. The angels of nature are always around...spinning yarns in the clouds, turning stones underground. They gently reveal the ways of faith. Like bits of heaven, they show us God's face.

The Crystal Heart Jewel

"What a busy weekend," Jane thought to herself as she slumped in a canvas chair next to a crackling evening fire alongside the beach. She always enjoyed camping with her husband and two children, yet she was thoroughly exhausted. They never ended a camping excursion without exploring every nook and cranny of the surrounding terrain. "What a way to relax!" she thought to herself sarcastically as she reviewed the activity-packed day in her mind. She silently wondered if tomorrow would hold as many chores.

"Here, Mom, have a marshmallow!" insisted her daughter as she abruptly broke into her thoughts. "I made it just the way you like. Burned!" she exclaimed.

Jane smiled and grabbed the charcoal marshmallow from a dirty stick. She realized as she tasted the crispy treat that her life in many ways had become a lot like this marshmallow—she was burned out! If only she could muster more energy for the kids. Her career obligations seemed to drain every ounce of her spirit; and by the weekend, she found herself numb and empty.

Jane, not unlike many working mothers, felt pangs of guilt frequently, due to an inability to fully give her attention to her children. This usually caused overcompensation in her mother role as she tried desperately to fulfill it during her time away from the office. Although Jane performed supermom tasks daily, she lacked the natural ability that some moms have to be there for their children, both in mind and spirit.

"Would you like another marshmallow, Mommy?" asked Jane's son, trying hard to please.

"No, thank you, I'm quite full," replied Jane as she scooped him up in her tired, aching arms. "I love you, you know," Jane whispered in his warm little ear.

They all sat for several more minutes together by the blazing fire. Its red hot tentacles rose in pointed patterns in an array of snapping peaks that filled the blackness of the night. The kids eyes began to droop as they watched the last log collapse in a smolder of white dust.

"We had best get to sleep," Dad suggested after the fire had completely burned out. "Tomorrow will be another fun day."

Inside the nylon dome tent, they rested on lumpy sleeping bags and hand-stitched blankets. Serenaded by a chorus of crickets, Jane quietly wondered before she drifted off to sleep just how much fun her husband meant. She was so exhausted, it would be nice to have one full day to relax and recuperate before Monday's schedule began again.

The family woke the next morning to the rushing sound of crashing waves pounding the large rocks that surrounded the beach.

"It's really windy today," Dad declared as Jane and the children stepped out of the tent. "Would you like some coffee, sweetie?"

"Yes, please," Jane accepted groggily.

While they drank coffee at an old wooden picnic table, Jane's husband told her he met some neighbors that morning and invited them over to visit.

"They have three boys," he said, "and I was thinking they might want to play with our kids."

Jane responded in a bitter voice, "Great, we get two days together, and you invite people over we don't even know!"

"You'll see. They are very nice, sweetie," her husband reassured her.

After the regular camping routine of tidying up after breakfast, sure enough, over trotted a strange family of five. They smoked cigarettes, which did not settle well with Jane at all considering she was trying to give up the habit. They all seemed rather loud and obnoxious; however, Jane did her best to tolerate their company.

After what seemed like an extended hour of visiting, the children decided they wanted to go on a treasure hunt. The campground was embedded with dips and gullies, perfect for burying hidden treasure.

"Do you have anything they could use for treasure?" Jane's husband asked her as he began drawing a secret treasure map on a leftover napkin.

Jane shuffled impatiently through her oversized purse and pulled out pieces of change, old buttons, a safety pin, a small bottle of perfume, and a crystal heart shaped jewel.

"Here you go," she said. "Use these!"

Dad excitedly hurried off to bury the secret treasure as the kids huddled around the napkin with the discover map. After a minute or two, he returned with a happy smirk on his face. He told the children they could begin searching the campground and warned them they would have the best luck sticking close to the map.

It never ceased to amaze Jane just how much energy her husband had for the kids. She was envious of his ability to participate in their fun. Laughing and playing like a child himself, he completely lost himself in games and fun activities.

Jane's thoughts of inferiority were broken by the sound of her daughter running toward her in tears. She ran up to the picnic bench where Jane was sitting and in a shattered voice explained that Jane had made a terrible mistake in assembling the secret treasure.

"What is wrong with the treasure?" Jane asked in puzzled concern.

"One of the other boys found it, and it contained the crystal heart jewel I gave you! It was supposed to be special! You said you would keep it forever!" she cried.

Immediately, Jane was filled with the remorse of having failed again in her attempts to be a good mom. It seemed she had a habit of never really listening to the needs and concerns of her children. She was there, but she was not.

"I'm so sorry," Jane admitted softly as she wrapped her little girl in her trembling arms. "There's nothing we can do about it now." Jane's eyes filled with tears of hopelessness as she cuddled her daughter with the distinct feeling she was never going to be able to get this "mom thing" right.

The camping excursion was the last one of summer, and soon the family entered the structured schedule of fall. School, sports, and friends kept the children very busy. Jane continued to achieve her successes in the boardroom by day and strived to make up for lost time with her children by night. This particular fall, Jane's thoughts turned more and more often to the realities she was daily facing. Like the colors of the leaves, Jane knew the colors of her life could not remain the same. She knew she could possess greater happiness. Her discomfort grew increasingly intense, and the time came during that blustery, cold winter when she resolved to fulfill her deepest desires and become a "real mom."

She gave an extended notice to the corporation so she could finish her responsibilities and obligations before entering "full-time mom-hood." That Easter was the first full weekend she had the opportunity to really get to know her children. The year passed—first came the green fingers of spring, and then, once again the warm pleasures of summer. With each passing day, Jane began to understand her children more completely. She gained the ability to listen—really listen—to their thoughts, concerns, and needs. She even discovered the blessing of sharing in their hopes and dreams.

Summer brought their first campout of the year. They packed suitcases, plastic plates and utensils, water and sand toys, even bicycles. Jane enjoyed having the extra time to pack items that the children could enjoy. They arrived at the lake at dusk. After pitching the tent, they all lay under a blanket of twinkling stars by the glow of the campfire. Jane rested comfortably in her new role as a "real mom" verses the "supermom" want-to-be she once was.

Jane woke up early the next day, and as the sunrise painted the morning sky, she prepared to take the kids to a wonderful park near the campground. She fixed coffee for her husband as she began to hear her family stir inside the tent in sighs and giggles.

"I'm going to take you to a park this morning," she announced as the children ducked their heads out of the tent. They bounced and cheered in unison as Jane fixed them bacon and eggs over the grill for breakfast.

"Would you like to come, dear?" Jane asked her husband.

"No thanks, sweetie. You guys go and have fun," he recommended. He thought it was so nice to finally enjoy the radiant sounds of his wife's laughter along with the children's. She was finally learning to play like he did, and it tickled him to see Jane so joyful and free.

When they arrived at the park, the kids hopped out of the car to race to the huge wooden structures that wound their way up the trees. Jane strolled toward where they were playing and smiled to see how happy they were. She rested near the bridge where the kids stood swinging back and forth. There she reminisced in gratitude for days gone by. She felt so secure in her dedication to the children. Although they had realized a drastic reduction in income, God blessed them daily and continued to meet their needs.

Jane knew the rewards she could give her kids by staying home would far surpass any expectations she once had to be a financial provider.

Her thoughts were interrupted by the joyful screams of her daughter. As she glanced up toward the bridge, she saw her little girl skipping toward her with a huge smile of excitement.

"Mommy! Mommy!" she yelled in wonderment. "Look what I found!"

Jane gazed down into her daughter's open palm to discover the crystal heart jewel gleaming in the sun as it rested in her daughter's little hand. It was the exact jewel she had given away in the treasure hunt last summer.

"It's the crystal heart jewel I gave you to keep forever!" her daughter exclaimed. "It must have fallen out of that boy's pocket at this same park last year. Can you believe it, Mommy? It waited right here for you all year!"

Jane's eyes swelled in warm tears of thankfulness. The crystal heart jewel was her special sign from God that it had not been too late to begin again. She was given another opportunity to hold and keep that crystal jewel from her daughter, just as she was granted the opportunity to treasure her children like the sparkling jewels they are.

Jane deepened her understanding of life and "mom-hood" that day as she slowly grew in wisdom to know the difference between "juggling kids as another item that must be managed" and "dedicating her life to the spirit of their being." Like the crystal heart jewel her daughter gave her for safe-keeping long ago, her children were special jewels from heaven above, given to her to treasure for a lifetime.

It was reassuring to see that God would provide her the opportunity to treasure the crystal heart jewel again, just as He had freely given her another chance to be the mom she had always wanted to be! Not a "super-mom," but a mom who truly cherishes the hearts of her children.

Meet Me by the Apple Tree

I woke up Monday morning to wake my kids for school. I helped them bundle up; the weather was getting cool.

I poured their cereal in a bowl. They ate as I read the prayer verse scroll.

My daughter asked before we left, a question I later pondered in depth: "I wonder if you'd meet me after school, on the trail that runs by the pool...

Would you meet me under the apple tree?"

Now, at first I paused in hesitance. I asked them to walk alone, work was intense.

I said "I'll try," and that was that, the day unfolded and later I sat...
Under the apple tree.

You see no matter what I do, I am a mom. Life is life, and life goes on.
My children, they complete my soul. Their love runs free; they make me whole.

To build them is my biggest chore; despite the rest, they are my core.

Teaching them in faith must come first; without this gift, all else is cursed.

And so I meet them every day, and before bed, we kneel and pray.

"Now I lay me down to sleep. I pray the Lord my soul to keep. If I should die before I wake, I pray the Lord my soul to take."

That night my mind drifted from their small voices, as I wished to God out of all my choices...

He would always help this "busy me" find time to meet them by the apple tree.

The Plastic Pipes

It was a scorching day, in the midst of a summer drought. My family and I were traveling to San Diego, California, to luxuriate in my in-law's home. Their house was comparable to a Victorian mansion, decorated in antiques and fine silken draperies. It contained more artifacts than a museum and held more collectibles than an antique shop. Each room promenaded in a quaint touch of richly threaded quilts and painted prints that each told a special story. It was an ideal place of escape and refreshment—almost like a bed and breakfast resort.

My husband's father was an antique dealer, which accounted for most of the luxurious decor. His mother appreciated the finer things of life, which increased their enjoyment of their home. Despite their grand taste, they always made us feel very comfortable and welcome. They placed more quilt feather pillows on our bed then our heads could rest upon and prepared gourmet cuisine for every meal.

I found it amazing, at times, that my husband was born into this family, yet he had such a natural simplicity about him. He inherited his mother's unique ability to sensitively care for others. My husband knows me better than I know myself. He was born with the kindness of an angel and a heart of the Lord.

It was sometimes difficult for me to completely accept the loving traits of my husband, coming from a lifetime of pain and sorrow, most of which was self-inflicted. I did not always feel like I deserved his royal treatment. Although I adored his gentle nature, I was haunted by the fear that someday he would discover my hidden burdens. Wedged deepest in my soul was the pain of losing my father at an early age. Although he had his defects, he was my best friend. When he died, a part of me died.

After resting and dining for two days with my husband's parents, we decided to join his father on an antique excursion. We accompanied him to an enormous auction where we spent a day surrounded by dusty boxes of old treasures with people swarming around them like busy bees around hives of honey. My husband and I found a small space in the middle of a anxious crowd where we stood until the auctioneer was ready to begin his rattling march through the sale of each old piece. I couldn't help but wonder what exactly was so intriguing about "old stuff"?

Several curious looking assistants took turns displaying each item as the auctioneer rambled his coaxing dance of promotion. The sweat beaded on our foreheads as we patiently waited for my father-in-law to secure his bids. My mind began to funnel above the heat in remembrance of days past when my father retreated to his condo in San Diego. My dad was so much like my husband's father, an entrepreneur and dealer, although my dad dealt in politics rather than antiques.

Although I limited conversation about my dad in an attempt to hide my feelings of sorrow and loss, my husband seemed to understand my void. He understood the unexplainable. He read my soul like an open book. As my eyes wandered above the noisy crowd, he leaned over and gently kissed my cheek. I felt his arm wrap half way around me, and his hand rest smoothly against my stomach.

My attention was again drawn to the excitement of the crowd and the rattling auctioneer who, by this time, seemed to be about half finished in his attempt to place each dusty item in the hand of another. It was then that his fingers lifted a ring of walnut brown pipes engraved in black patterns. My eyes widened at first glance with the recollection of a ring of pipes my dad once kept on a shelf in his study at home. We used to chew on their plastic ends for hours as we sat writing side by side with a symphony playing on the radio. Most of the slots along the ring hung a full size pipe, but in the middle, sat a baby pipe, just my size.

I turned to my husband and shared my special memory of writing with my dad in his study as we chewed on plastic pipes. "Pretty stupid, huh?" I said after I had opened up a small part of the hole in my heart. "No, not at all," he responded as I felt his hand stroke my back in circles of comfort.

Before I realized what he was doing, my husband pulled his hand from behind my back and raised it to bid on the ring of plastic pipes. "What are you doing? We don't smoke. We don't need a set of pipes," I insisted as he continued to bid as the price of the pipe set rose. He paused only to turn and say, "Yes, we do."

My husband soon won the contest of bidding, and the auctioneer's assistant came over to place the ring of plastic pipes in my husband's hands. He refused the pipes with a smile and said they were for me. The plump man smirked and shrugged his shoulders as he handed me the pipes. Tears flowed down my smiling cheeks and onto the center of the ring of pipes, where my baby pipe once sat. I could not speak words of gratitude; my throat was tied in a knot of emotions.

My husband handed me both restoration of my past and a promise for the future with that ring of plastic pipes. I suddenly knew completely that he could help fill the hole of sorrow in my heart—he could mend that empty place that once knew my dad's love. God was filling my void through a small token of His love, given to me thoughtfully through the hands of my partner and friend. My soul had finally found another to share my pain. My heart had found another to share my love. My spirit had found another to help show me freedom.

Faithful Impressions

Majestic warmth swells round the heart. Evergreen love draws near and apart.

The wind dances between both ends, in eternal breath, a message it sends.

Guided steps, patterned imprints, good deeds. Following footprints in prayer, the impressions we leave.

Weathered tide, soft confession, fragile action in faith. Golden memories, silver promises, sequenced in timeless space.

Where love is held, the priceless treasure shone. Fear not, step in faith; we are never alone.

Promises Upon My Heart

My heart pounded abnormally fast in episodes of tachycardia toward the end of the horrible decade I spent lost in the grip of alcoholism. I couldn't survive the pain found within my days without the comfort of several glasses of wine. Even though I had lost my mother to alcoholism, it didn't seem to matter. I had sunk so far down into my addiction that there seemed to be no way out. I knew deep down my only hope was in sobriety, yet the thought of giving up my only source of what I illusively called "peace" knotted my stomach with fear.

My last days drinking turned my depression into deeper hopelessness. I became painfully aware of the end of the path that I blindly stumbled towards. The one thing that prevented me from continuing to slowly kill myself was my kids. The pain I felt having witnessed my own mother's death was fresh in my mind. I could not put my children through the horror I experienced through the years, watching my mom slowly drink her life away.

Now it was New Year's Eve, almost ten years later, and here I sit with a circle of friends. Thankfully, through a series of difficult events, I had asked God to show me a better way of life. Not only did He relieve me of my desire to drink, He led me to a fellowship of friends whom I could identify with; they shared my pain. I originally began recovering from alcoholism to simply live long enough to see my kids through school; but through the last five years, I was blessed with a love for myself that I never knew before.

The dark path I once traveled had been colored by the hands of people just like the ones who sat around this circle. The first of many wonderful friends in recovery handed me a list of promises. Each promise was hand marked on a large poster board upon a painted heart. It was the most intriguing heart I had ever seen. It was so full of life; it was plump full of contentment. The poster was designed in hope. I hung it on my refrigerator, even though the words seemed foreign and unachievable. I had no idea the colors of my inner landscape would be transformed into a beauty that would grant me every promise upon that heart.

Sitting in the circle, I reviewed the passing year in my mind before the discussions began. So much was happening in my life. God's miracles had shown me a whole new world. I found the courage to change myself over the past year—a courage that, in the past, had always been squelched by fear. The 12 steps of recovery were helping me deepen my understanding of myself. With the help of another, I finally dared to explore my inner needs, hopes, and dreams. I gave in to the philosophy "God meets our needs as we seek to meet the needs of others." It seemed I could not give enough to help others. I even gave that beautiful poster of promises to one of the women I mentor who was approaching two years in her recovery from addiction.

The meeting was about to begin. The chairperson introduced herself. Then, she reached under her chair and pulled out a bundle of posters. As she unwrapped the bundle, I caught a glimpse of a familiar heart. *Could it be?* I thought to myself. It looked like the same poster of promises that once hung on my refrigerator. Although I was happy to place it in the hands of another, I missed the poster each time I noticed the bare space on my refrigerator where it once hung.

Sure enough, I could now clearly see the same handwritten promises. I knew it was the same poster. *How could this be?* I thought. This meeting was on the other side of town, and it was another friend who initially gave me that special gift to hang. The poster was handmade, not commercially generated. I picked one up with great curiosity. As I reread the promises written upon the heart in amazement, I can honestly say I felt them resident upon my heart that day. What initially seemed to be a list of ideas foreign and unattainable now served as a confirmation of my hope and "real peace."

I held the poster tightly in gratitude throughout the meeting that day. Afterwards, I approached the chairperson. Her name was Allison. I told her that years ago I hung that same poster on my refrigerator, given to me by another, and in the past year I had given it to someone else who needed it more. I told her how much I had missed it. Allison smiled and told me she was the artist. “Now you can hang this one in its place.”

I was reminded that day of the many gifts we find in God’s world. So many things have happened in my life since I began healing, seemingly small coincidences that were truly gifts from God. Friendship and fellowship are only two of the many gifts that help God’s miracles shine! I have learned that giving, like the well of love, never runs dry. God continues to replenish me, just as He replaced my poster, as I seek to meet the needs of others along my journey.

My recovery from addiction, which began in an effort to survive long enough to see my kids through school, has grown into an eternal way of living that hands me new dreams daily. God’s promises have filled my days with abundant blessings. My heart, once haunted by the pounding recollection of a horrible past, now flutters freely like the wings of a butterfly. My mind, once trapped in a castle of despair, now reaches toward the wisdom of tomorrow. My soul, once lost, now guides each of my days as I contribute to my destiny.

In God's Grace

Dear God, please help me by listening to my need.
For comfort and protection; for I am just a seed.

Daily chores are naught, separate from your love.
Your tender care and guidance, precious from above.

Help me grow and teach me; flowers need the rain.
Soothe my heart in sadness. Your love softens pain…

As the sunset slowly fades 'cross an apricot field.
Petals bed in the dew of night, tomorrows seeds to yield.

Lord, help me stay near You, each and every day.
Help me stay near You always, in Jesus' name I pray.

Amen

A Crayon in a Globe

There rests on a light oak book stand a dark orange crayon, broken in half and jammed into the pencil-sharpening hole designed in the base of a tiny globe of the world. This tarnished copper globe was manufactured as an office showpiece but with utility in mind. Resting on a busy desk, it reminded many tired business workers that a whole world existed outside of their small cubicle space. One could pause while sharpening a pencil to spin this tiny globe with its painted patches of land and loosen the mind in an exploration of broader horizons.

One day, as the globe sat unattended on a wooden desk, a child and her mother came into the office to visit an employee. The mom, bubbly and consumed in delightful conversation, lost track of her child who began inquisitively roaming the office. The child searched the busy, paper crowded office until her small hands rested on the globe. She picked it up in fascination as her blue eyes watched the world as it twirled in her hand.

After twirling it for awhile, she grew bored and reached inside her pocket. Maneuvering her fingers to the bottom, she found a paper covered crayon. Pulling it out, she saw that it was worn flat and unusable. Eyes lighting up, she decided to sharpen it. She grabbed the crayon, pulled it out, and twisted it into the hole of the sharpener at the base of the globe. Its tight fit frustrated the child as she more furiously tried to jam in the crayon. Before long, the crayon snapped in two, half remaining stuck in the copper base.

The child began to cry as she glanced between half of the orange crayon she clutched in one hand, and the other half that was stuck in the hole of the globe. Her mother finally broke away from her conversation and ran over to see why her little girl was crying. She was embarrassed to discover the crayon broken and jammed into the office globe. She swept it from the hands of her child and apologetically brought it to the man behind the desk where she shamefully offered to have the crayon removed.

The man behind the desk chuckled as he took the globe. He walked over to the child who still stood in tears. He knelt down beside her and assured her in a soothing voice that she had caused him no harm. "I don't have any children of my own," he said. "My wife and I have been waiting for several years. We keep praying and trusting that God will bless us with the gift of a baby when the time is truly right. I will keep this crayon stuck in my globe and display it as a reminder that some day our prayers will be answered. I indeed look forward to their having the same curiosity as you do!"

The mother and her child listened to the man empathetically as they realized that what they thought was an act of destruction could be used as a special gift of hope. They finished their business and departed with thankfulness at his generosity. The man shut the door of the office as he turned to glance down again at the tiny copper globe stuck with an orange crayon. He spun it round and round like the child had done earlier, watching the orange crayon as the world twisted by. How he hoped his prayers indeed would be answered one day.

Five years later, the same tarnished copper globe with the same dark orange crayon jammed into a small hole in its base rests on a light oak bookshelf. Beside the bookshelf sits a dark, wooden rocking chair with a well-used gold padded seat. The office man took the globe home with him the day it became a symbol of his dream to come. He set it carefully on the top shelf with the crayon facing outward. Several guests throughout the past five years offered to remove the crayon for him, but he insisted to each one that the crayon must remain.

In the past few days, he has often glanced at the tiny globe when he feeds his newborn baby in the rocking chair. He will never forget the small child who brought him a symbol of hope for the future to remind him that God would someday answer his prayers. Her presumed recklessness in the office turned out to be a gift from God, packaged in the smallness of a fine artifact. The globe will remain through the years—crayon untouched—the hope it symbolized now imprinted in the hearts of many.

Don't Stand in the Way of a Miracle

Miracles bring hope as they highlight special days.
I enjoy their mystic beauty when I don't stand in the way.
Sometimes I try to help too much, loosing sight of my small part.
I forget that God works wonders through the whispers of my heart.
Sometimes I try and try some more until all hope seems gone.
It's not before I'm exhausted that I hear the quiet song:

"A miracle will grace us when the time is truly right.
The beauty of God's handiwork is perfect in His sight.
Each painful thing we see is part of a bigger plan.
His love and kindness never end when guided by His hand.
Grace is thread throughout the world to complete His tapestry.
Although I am part of a miracle, they don't begin with me."

I've spent many years of my life standing in the way.
I've tried and tried and tried some more when all I can do is pray.
Yet, life is filled with lessons; this may be the biggest one.
I will rest in peace every time when the miracle is done.

Spring Blossoms

My heart longs for the blossoms of spring. Her petals shed fragrant whispers of nature's renewal into the fresh breeze. Spring's blossoms scent my soul in the natural perfume of peace. Like the flower cupped in silence before her bloom, I replenish myself in the depths of my soul. Spring's delicately painted colors awake a sleepy heart in the dreams of tomorrow and cleanse the spirit of the troubles found in yesterday.

Winter's frosty bite often dulls the heart with a sour kiss of anxiety, fear, loneliness, and depression. God's gifts of nature seem to smother under layers of ice and deadened fields. Yet an eternal flame continues to warm the ones who live in the heart of their dreams—the precious dreams revealed to them through the window of the quiet soul.

Spring's blossoms provide the refreshment we long for. Their tender beauty and heavenly scent capture the heart and unite us with the heart of the earth. They replenish us to finish our journey. A deep breath of the tree's painted fingers blossoms the heart in true inner beauty. I become one with the Spirit in this special place of rebirth. Nature's fingers set my spirit free to spread my wings like an eagle. I fly in the reflections of my passionate soul in the eternal mirror nature holds in her hands.

Spring's blossoms help the soul touch eternity. Her colors decorate our sometimes colorless paths. The fingers of each tree lift tiny-blossomed treasures that remind me of God's miraculous nature. His world bears color and fruit. His blossoms can shine through my spirit to color a world of darkness. His fragrance can sustain me. Through His tender touch, I can reach to those around me in the spirit of the One who holds each petal of my soul. Just as these petals bring peace, I can blossom to the world in inner beauty. I can blossom in the mirror of who I am…a child of God.

Fill My Cup With Heaven

My eyes are hollowed in the shavings of ice that cover this world, as a cold blanket of evil steals one last gasp of air before returning to its deadened state of loneliness.
Yet, when I seal my silken eyelids, I am again warmed by the Son who warms all suns.
An eternal Light sheds upon my forehead.
A warm glow of peace shines upon my heart.
The frail nudity and bitter taste of winter buries only those whose spirits reside below the painted sky, for the warmth of summer is born within the soul that reaches beyond its worldly confines.
A hope stronger than the icy beads of despair reigns free in the spirit that truly seeks Thee.
Upon opening my tired lashes again, still the earth remains covered in life's cold damp blanket of pain. The teeth of the wind bite through flesh and shackle its game. Sinful frost carries poison, patterning jagged crystals of discomfort on a horizon that shelters the barren.
Only One Love escapes the desolate structures of nature's winter prey.
Only One Light can penetrate the ices of inhumanity.
Resting my weary eyes once more upon the Love of my heart and the Light of my spirit, I retreat through the window of my soul to reunite with the One who holds all hope.
His transcending warmth melts the icy beads that insulate the earth from His joy.
His love restores a fullness of spirit. Eternity begins and ends in the circle of His presence. His ultimate glory will clothe the emptiness of the land.
Blessed be my Father. Fill my cup with heaven.

Carnations for a Friend

People don't always realize just how important their gifts to others can be, especially during times of need. Many are reserved in their giving. Face it, most of us hold back the gifts of time, friendship, sharing, and caring until we are reasonably sure what's in it for us. There are some, however, who truly reach out from the depths of their heart, where giving freely is naturally born.

Carol is a perfect example of someone who shares unconditionally with others. It wasn't until she suffered a bout of cancer that she fully understood the art of giving without expectations of return. When she found out the lump in her breast was malignant, she was so overcome by depression and fear that she needed the support of others to help her through each day. The unconditional friendship and love of others helped her through the dark, fearful tunnel of her unknown health status. The special people who offered her gifts of time, conversation, and even household help embroidered a path of friendship that she could follow to recovery.

Five years later, Carol still remembers these special givers of love and support as if they were by her side yesterday. Through a blessing from God and as a result of their prayers, comfort, and fellowship, she has lived each of her days in wellness and remission. Now Carol understands intimately the necessity of being there for others in their struggles and needs. She has joined those who function from the depths of their soul to touch the hearts and lives of others. Although inhibited in previous years by an uncertainty in her ability to give to others anything of value, she now realizes that God has a way of showing her just what someone truly needs.

Carol especially encouraged one of the younger women she was supporting through some difficult times of change. This woman had been calling Carol daily for love and emotional support. Although Carol worked 55 hours a week and was head of her household, she always took time out from her busy schedule to lend an ear and offer heartfelt advice. Well over a year, she talked with this young woman on the phone and met with her for coffee and a hug.

Once again this young woman's birthday approached, and Carol searched her heart for a meaningful gift for her friend. That morning, Carol was doing her grocery shopping in a rush, when her eyes happened to rest upon a delicate bouquet of 12 miniature carnations tipped in rose color. She knew immediately they would make a lovely gift for her friend.

When Carol arrived at home with her groceries, she quickly picked up the phone and began dialing the young woman's number, while stuffing groceries in the cupboards with her free hand. After several rings at the other end of the line, Carol heard a rather empty, "Hello?" She invited the young woman to coffee that evening. She wanted the gift to be a surprise.

The young woman hedged and said she was suffering from severe depression that particular day. "I believe it is best for me to be alone today," she replied.

With the intention of surprising her with the carnations, Carol gently insisted that the young woman meet her anyway. She convinced her it might cheer her mood.

Later that evening, Carol arrived at the coffee shop where the two of them always met. She glanced from table to table to find her friend already there, sitting at a table in a dark corner of the restaurant. Carol placed the carnations behind her back and slowly approached the table. Little did she know, she was the only friend this young woman had.

Carol smiled and pulled the flowers from behind her back. The young woman met the bouquet with large teardrops that melted her stoic face. She certainly was not used to receiving birthday gifts. The two sat and held hands as Carol wished her a happy birthday and told her that her own birthday was just the day before. The young woman's eyes lit with a sparkle of happiness when Carol told her that their birthdays were just one day apart. Carol was touched that it seemed to bring her joy.

The young woman placed the bouquet of miniature carnations in her finest crystal vase when she returned home. She took one out and gave it to her daughter to keep in her bedroom. Her carnations stood tall for days upon days and never did wilt. They simply dried in a perfectly delicate form. Every time the young woman walked by the vase in her home, she paused to remember their special birthday meaning. They symbolized to her the birthday of her friend, rather than her own.

A year passed and it became the day before the young woman's birthday. She woke early and took her daughter and the dried bouquet of carnations on a drive out into the country. They passed through corn stalked horizons and row upon row of bales of hay before arriving at their destination. She pulled the car alongside a dirt road that wound its way to an old cemetery where she had laid her brother to rest years before. That day would have been his 30th birthday. They never knew their parents but had grown up together in an orphanage. Her brother had been her best and only friend.

She carefully stepped out of the car with the dried bouquet in her hand. Her daughter was still sleeping in the back seat. She unsteadily approached the headstone that bore her brother's name etched in the colors of the sunset. She slowly kneeled by his gravesite and with shaking hands, placed the dried flowers on his grave. Her weary eyes were lifted that day from the loneliness of his gravesite up towards the heavens above. Hope began to flicker, and it seemed as though the wind blew through her spirit, renewing her in the comfort of her newfound friendship.

Carol never knew how very much her gift of carnations actually meant in healing the heart of her friend. On the day of the gift, the young woman was still mourning the loss of her brother, whose birthday would have been the day before. Carol's birthday just happened to be on the same day as the young woman's brother's. It was as if God had given Carol the assignment of helping Him mend the wounded heart of this lonely woman by nudging her to give the gift that meant the beginning of healing.

The dried carnations scattered day after day in the hollow winds of the open field. The young woman did not visit the cemetery as frequently as in years past. She spent most of her time now enjoying her daughter and her newfound gift of friendship. She is grateful that Carol is a part of her life. Thank God for that special place in the core of our hearts that nudges us to give freely. Thank Him also for the whispers of our soul, which continually encourage us to love.

The Whispers of Your Soul

God? So far above the world it seems...All those times, why did you carry me? I've not shone as my light should be! I drifted from you. Didn't you see?

His gentle voice replied, "My child, I gave you a choice. For through My Son is born new life. He was with you in the dark valley. He paid the price."

I said, "That's fine and dandy. I'm glad you can forgive. In my mind, my past deserves no reprieve. Please let me be to live."

God said, "There is much more in life, than simply to survive." He challenged me to explore myself, "It is time to come alive!"

I argued, "You must be confused. I've never been a saint! My actions have fallen short of fate. My memories you did not paint."

God reminded me with His tender touch, He doesn't get confused. He set my faith in Him aglow. I began to realize in Him, I cannot lose.

I surrendered with a needed prayer, for alone I knew I'd flop. I begged for the courage to follow His will and let my selfishness drop.

He said, "My will is in your dreams, those dearest to your heart. The quiet whispers of your soul will make a beautiful start."

I began by stepping back through time, to when I was a child. My dreams I'd hung up long ago, further squelched by days run wild.

My Father said, "The time has come, to join me in our dreams. Affirm them, follow them; you will see, you're very special to me."

I joined my creative purpose, despite my inner doubt. And in His will He lifted me, beyond my feeble shouts.

God has shown me through a growing faith, His miraculous path of love. He shows me in my daily life, He's not so far above.

Blue Hearts

It takes a considerable amount of time, patience, genuine care, and concern to really know a child. Some parents today find themselves guilty of a lack of motivation in one or more of these crucial areas or simply suffer from a failure to fully realize the significant commitment of raising children. Joan was a prime example of a seemingly perfect mother who wound up in a "performance trap" in her career while her children were still young. The result was that year after year she slipped further and further from truly understanding the inner personalities and needs of her kids.

Like most kids, Joan's children Abby and Ben loved their mother despite the emotional distance they experienced from her and the numerous childcare providers they had had. They made the best of the time they spent together and tried to minimize thoughts of having a better relationship with Joan. Although she was being the best mom she could be at the time, there remained a special place deep in her heart that longed to give her children more. She carried a place of emptiness that could not be filled by the fringe benefits and perks of a successful career.

Another winter spread its blanket of frigid whiteness over the landscape, a garment that this year chilled Joan's personality and disposition. School activities flipped by constantly as the pages of the calendar turned, until a special day of revelation came in Joan's life. It was after another hectic day in the office that she raced down the freeway to whip her children out of day care. There was a long list of errands that still had to be accomplished before dinner and evening activities. She quickly helped the children fasten their coats before they rushed from day care to continue the journey home.

On their way to the grocery store, Ben began telling Joan about his day. He gleefully shared a long list of projects he was working on. His words bounced unheard against the windows of their racing car as they echoed unnoticed in Joan's mind, which was consumed in busy thought. In sensing her canned responses, Ben tucked his head inside the fur lining of his coat and squinted his eyes shut in disappointment. Abby reached over and touched his small back. She knew of his need for comfort and attention.

The car came to a screeching halt in the parking lot of the store. Joan held their hands tightly as she quickly pulled them along toward the automatic doors. With Abby on one side of her cart and Ben on the other, she rushed through the aisles throwing enough food in the basket to get them by for a couple more days. After they hurriedly canvassed the store and reached the checkout line, Joan let the children each pick out a treat.

They finally returned home after completing as many errands as time allowed. Leaving their home Monday through Friday every week at 6:00 A.M. made for homesick kids by 6:00 P.M. Joan's conscience frequently nagged at her when she took the time to notice the pale looks on her children's faces. Abby had even come up with a helpful phrase that she recited to her mom in hope of capturing her attention. "Don't hurry, don't worry!" she would remind Joan.

Well, this particular evening, upon their arrival in the kitchen, Joan was overcome by the revolutionary realization that the lives of her children were passing her by. Her head pounded as she feverishly stirred the hamburger in the skillet. The soft sounds of her children playing in the next room slowly began to seep through her emotional distance. The giggles of Abby and Ben began chipping away at her hardened disposition like a pick chipping away on a hard surface of ice.

Joan dropped the spatula into the skillet and looked at the dinner she had been stirring in a frenzy. Her burning eyes looked above the stove and followed the delicately designed blue hearts that bordered the paper at the top of her kitchen. She followed the blue hearts as her heart followed their pattern right to the door of the kitchen leading into the living room where the children giggled. Her heart skipped a beat as she turned the stove off and went to join the children in their play. She sat down next to her kids, and for the first time in years focused completely on them. Her head slowly quit pounding, and her spirit lightened as she sat in a circle with them playing hand games.

Dinner was served late that evening. Joan bathed the kids before bed and gathered them in her room for a story. She hadn't read to them since they were very little. Ben hugged her tightly on one side, and Abby lay right against her on the other. Like sponges that had been left to dry, they soaked up their mother's love with open and forgiving arms. After the story, Joan lay between them until they both fell asleep. Feeling a deep peace as the result of this inner change in attitude, she closed her tired eyes to do the only thing she knew to do when she needed help—pray.

That night, Joan lifted everything she had to the heavens, which didn't seem like much. Little did she know that God had already created a path for her to follow by which she could begin to really get to know her children again. He had already prepared a plan for healing her sad heart.

Joan felt an inner nudge over the following days, a quiet urge in her soul that challenged her to reprioritize her life and spend more time with her children. She discussed this revolution of thought, as well as her concerns, with her husband who guaranteed he would support her in any decisions she must make. Her task in the days to come would be to deepen her trust in God's plan for their lives. It seems life has a way of pressing us deeper in faith as we open our hearts to the guidance of God. Joan knew it was time to make major changes.

After praying for the courage to change daily and sometimes hourly for months, Joan resigned her position and put her career on hold. She warned the family that they would face a drastic reduction in the household budget, but no one seemed to mind. They all confessed they would rather have her time and attention than her salary. Tears from heaven trickled down her face and washed her worried cheeks in affirmation. Joan was destined to be a full-time mom, and the anticipation of having the time to really get to know her kids swelled in her heart with happiness.

That summer, Joan spent time getting to know her children in a way that encompasses the spirit completely. They went swimming, hiking, bike riding, roller skating; they had picnics, raised bunnies, and planted flowers. Most importantly, they did all of these activities *together*. Joan gained the ability to listen closely to the needs of her children, both emotional and physical. She learned of her significant role as mother and provider of time and attention in her children's lives, rather than wearing herself thin in an attempt to provide for them financially.

Joan's children are grown now. Ben and Abby both have children of their own. Joan returned to her career when they completed high school. Joan and her husband do not live in the fanciest home in the neighborhood; in fact, their living is quite modest. They chose to make certain sacrifices when Joan became a stay-at-home mother. They do have a nice porch swing on the front patio, however, where Joan rests in the evening after a hectic day in the office. As she glides back and forth in the evening breeze, her sweet memories echo the soft sounds of laughter from her children as they all played together in the circle. All of the money in the world could not replace the golden values she personally instilled in the developing souls of her children.

Joan made a bold decision in her life—she decided to take the time to really get to know her children. She exited a thriving career to build their hearts and minds in faith. Somewhere, along this path, she forgot what it was like to "hurry and worry." She was relieved from the bondage of her "performance trap," and handed the key to eternity, which lies in the hand of God. Joan is grateful for her transformation.

Now, as her spirit is lifted toward the velvety clouds that bid each other goodnight on an apricot horizon, she does not regret one day. For it was the early days of rushing and overachieving in the wrong areas that prepared her heart for change, and then all of the beautiful days followed when she appreciated the important lessons she had learned.

The Ballad of Time

Time dances on and on.
She spins, she swirls, her toes upon...
Hearts and lives in the wind,
Spirits free, released from sin.

Time's wonders never cease.
Her delicacy and beauty restore peace.
Souls lifted, joined in prayer.
Parched hearts begin to care.

The ballad of time provides a taste.
Her hungers long the eternal place,
Where her spirit completes and fills her soul.
Her satisfaction is turned to an infinite whole.

She lifts and guides us in His loving arms.
When we join in the dance, we uncover her charms.
As we spin and swirl, arms stretched above,
The dance is complete in the graces of love.

A Porcelain Angel

When I was young, my grandma gave me an angel carved in delicate porcelain. The angel held her pale blue skirt with one hand, and in the other she held a stone of turquoise, which is my birthstone. I treasured this angel through the years, as my grandmother and I drifted away from each other in the midst of several of life's misunderstood events.

You see, when I was young, my parents divorced. Coming from a broken family seemed to set me outside of the usual family circle. I felt like the black sheep. In my early years of adulthood, I failed miserably at trying to build a functional home life for myself. Having very low self-esteem, I continued to chose mates who were abusive. My unhealthy relationship patterns left me divorced twice. When I married a third time, finally to someone caring and sincere, and no one from the family circle—including my grandma—came to our wedding, I knew for sure I was considered the black sheep.

Knowing deep down that it was beyond my power to explain to my grandma all of the reasons for my many mistakes and broken marriages, I let go of our relationship and placed it in the hands of God. That summer at a garage sale I held, I put up for sale the porcelain angel she had given me as a child. I only marked it a dime, knowing another child may find the comfort I once did in this special treasure. It only brought me the pain of once precious memories of my grandma that now were gone.

The porcelain angel sold that summer, and the fall leaves faded into a winter of miracles in my life. One of the beautiful gifts I received during that incredible winter came in the form of another angel. After all of the years I felt distant from my grandma, she finally learned the depth of my early struggles and the pain I had endured in abusive relationships. God re-opened the door through which she could care for me.

It was only after I had accepted completely in my heart her misunderstanding of my circumstances that things began to change. As I let go of my need to convince her that I was a good person even though I had been divorced twice, God began to show her my true character in a way that touched her soul. She read a story of the details of my upbringing and experiences in abusive relationships and finally understood me.

One day, as I walked up the entry stairs of our home and turned into the kitchen, I noticed a huge stack of mail. I sorted through it in the usual manner, until I came to a lightweight package. Curious, I broke open the tape and gently lifted the top of the wrapping. It was a porcelain plate, carved in the shape of the wings of an angel and painted upon it was an angel in a pale blue dress. Her long golden hair was dressed in violets and daisies, which blew in the wind with her wings. She came with a certificate of authenticity that revealed her name, "Serenity's Song."

My eyes began to swell in tears as I opened the card that came with this beautiful gift. It was a note from my grandma. She said she loved me and was proud to have me for a granddaughter. Little did she know, I had sold my porcelain angel who held the turquoise stone of my birth, after dusting it for years in my many broken homes. She was now replacing her with the gift of serenity, a blessing I was finally able to enjoy.

I still wonder sometimes about the new home of my angel with the turquoise stone, as I continue to experience gratitude for all of the relationships God has restored in my life, including the one with my grandmother. For me, my birthstone was exchanged for the wings of freedom as the petals of my life blow in a breeze of peace and serenity. I hope others who suffer from broken relationships can find the gifts of healing I have discovered along my journey. I have been blessed with an authenticity of my own. I, too, sing a song of serenity.

Home With Great Grandma

Lavender lay upon her face,
like the faint iris pales its place.

Her heart is filled with glory.
The sun sparkles behind her eyes, a bluebird sings
and sometimes cries.

Her spirit is filled with giving.
Flowers curl each strand of hair,
the depths of beauty everywhere.

Her mind dwells in eternity.
The meadows spill from her open hand,
like a wing spread above the land.

Her soul belongs to destiny.
Parted by the hands of time,
she waits in faith until a special time...

When wings are joined in unity.
So they can fly through the pearly gate,
home at last at the end of fate.

Blessed together in heaven.

The Pincock Van

There once was a large family of 11—a mom and dad and nine children. They lived in a house the size of any ordinary house. One would find it hard to imagine exactly how they fit everyone in bed. This family of 11 owned one vehicle, a blue and white van that seldom rested in the driveway. It was constantly circling the neighborhood either for work, school, church, or other family activities. It would be hard to approximate just how many miles that van had travelled; yet, it faithfully took them from point A to point B day after day for years and years.

The Pincocks were a close family; of course, you would have to be close to fit 11 members in one ordinary house and one blue and white van. Despite their scrunched quarters, you would never catch a Pincock without a smile. Whether in the yard or peeking their head out of the window of the van, a splendid radiance surrounded the eyes of every Pincock. Their faces delivered messages of contentment and praise.

One might guess that their blue and white van would succumb to the hands of time that wore it down as the years and miles passed by, but to the contrary, its engine hummed a quiet tune of satisfactory performance every time it graced the streets. It continued to diligently carry the Pincocks through many seasons of change. It was as if it was one of the many vehicles God used to sustain them—a family of 11—living on the budget of one breadwinner. Mrs. Pincock stayed home full-time raising all of their children in the Spirit.

It was most common to see the eldest daughter driving behind the large, upright wheel of the van. Her name was Kristyn, and being the oldest of a family of nine children, she often assumed the majority of the responsibilities, including taxicab driving. As seemed to be the Pincock tradition, she always adhered to the smiling face motto. One must wonder how a young girl with so much responsibility could always be so pleasant. Most people would be bothered by similar burdensome circumstances.

The day finally came for Krystin to go off to college. Her mom baked her several homemade graduation cakes and invited all of the neighbors for an open house. The blue and white van rested in the driveway for this special occasion. The guests were made to feel at home in the small rooms of their house as friends and family bid the oldest Pincock child farewell from her crowded nest.

The second child in age, their eldest son, assumed many of the responsibilities of the family, including driving the blue and white van of smiles. The van that once glided around corners with ease now left blackened skid marks as it occasionally screeched to a halt, yet the children were still carried safely to their destinations. It was probably hard for the family to get used to Krystin being away at school.

She decided to study to become a teacher, another amazing feature of this story. After spending years helping her mother raise eight children, she chose to continue in a field that allowed her to work with children. Her close upbringing evidently taught her of the important contribution children make to the world. She would close the door of helping her mother build her family by opening a larger and wonderful door into a life of helping build other children in the family of God.

The Pincock family saved for years to afford Krystin a car to take with her to college. It was a tiny boxcar with rust around the casings of the tires. Again, it seemed to do the job of getting her from point A to point B. It could be found every holiday parked in their driveway next to the blue and white van. And there it sat. Whenever Krystin visited home, she accompanied the rest of the family in the tight quarters of the van, each time resuming her position as driver with a smile.

This story proves that not all things in life must be glamorous to create happiness and satisfaction. God can even package contentment in the close confines of a simple house that holds 11, and a blue and white van that carries smiling faces day after day, as the years pass by. Some of the most basic forms of enjoyment are found in the family that stays close, through thick and thin. What some might view as unfortunate constraints often bring beauty and fullness to the lives of others as they serve as soul enriching experiences.

You may wonder now if the blue and white van will run forever. Mr. and Mrs. Pincock are gray and the van still delivers their family of smiling faces to and from their destination. You may even suspect that this family has a destiny beyond the well-beaten paths they travel in life through the years. Each of the miles they have journeyed hand in hand has brought them one corner closer to their place in eternity. Their simple home here on earth may someday be exchanged for a heavenly home with plenty of room for their humble souls, their blue and white van for the wings of a dove.

Where There Is God, There Is Love

Love can be found where a softly colored rainbow wraps its arms around a charcoal lake.

Love shines through the thick clouds as they break open on a rainy day giving way to beams of sunlight.

Love ripples circled reflections in an olive colored pond as a child tosses in a stone.

Love can be found in the gentle sunset that illuminates a sky of tender blues and pinks, easing the bite of darkness.

Where family comes together in a world of confusion and uniqueness, there is love.

Love is in the home where hearts beat together in understanding, trust, and honesty.

Where God is creating—above the stars, underneath flower petals, and inside seashells—love is there.

Where I found God, there I found love.

The Magic of a Garden

It was late May. Summer began to brush her warm spirit across the land as birds assembled their fresh nests and flowers opened their eyes to the sun. My vegetable garden found a fresh place on this season when the world glistened in the fullness of God's creation. I decided to move it to the far end of the yard that year, along the back fence, which borders our yard and the neighbor's. They had a vegetable garden also, colossal in comparison to ours. It was planted along the opposite side of the same wooden picket fence.

The early days of summer captured my thoughts with envy as I watered my modest garden. I longed for the financial resources to plant a larger garden myself. Each time I pulled the hose down to my small garden, I would stand as I watered it, admiring the garden of my neighbor. It was so lush and beautiful.

As the season unfolded on the wings of a scorching summer breeze, I began to notice the neighbor's garden wilt. I was initially pleased in selfishness that perhaps they would not realize an overabundance of vegetables, while we settled for smidgens. But after a few more days of blustering heat passed, my heart began to soften. One day, something inside of me changed as I caught myself drifting again in thoughts of envy. A soft breeze brushed a new outlook and attitude across my cheeks, one that I will cherish forever.

I turned my eyes from the neighbor's large, wilted garden to the hose that was still soaking the soil of my yard. My hand raised the hose as my arm lifted to resume watering by giving their garden a dash of water. Each day that followed, I watered the neighbor's garden after finishing my own. Before long, their vegetables and plants again began to flourish in the variegated beauty they once displayed.

This experience set my mind free of envy that summer, and my own garden began to spread like magic. The vegetables, originally confined to a small square in the far corner of the yard, reproduced and spread their fingers to cover a large rectangular area of space by summer's end. Each of my tomato plants yielded more than we could eat as a family. Caring for the neighbor's garden, that which I had once despised, changed both my own garden and my inner attitude so that both grew in abundance.

The magic of a garden is but one of the vessels by which God manifests His miracles and shows us His ways. When we truly love our neighbors as we do ourselves, we are released from the bondage of selfishness, which frees us to be God's people. When we seek to meet the needs of others, God miraculously and lovingly meets our own. The magic of a garden and God's eternal magic can be ours to cherish. In nourishing the seeds of others in the garden of the Lord, our own seeds will produce blossoms in spectacular beauty!

When God Gently Knocks

God gently knocks through the fallen colored leaves,
sequencing the trail before me in raindrops of inspiration.
Thoughts capture my mind as the Dream Catcher of life
speaks through the window of my quiet soul.
The coolness of the musty breeze winds fingers of freedom
through my hair, as I listen to the whispers of my heart.
Nature's tender touch brushes my spirit, painting
rainbow colors under the magic wand of God.
Love twists through the dampened tree, awakening her
branches in peaceful sprinkles of sunshine.
God gently knocks in the depths of life, satisfying query
in the crisp detail of nature's wonderment.
God gently knocks in the depths of a quiet soul;
He whispers through the delicacy of nature's brush.

Who Taught Your Child to Tie His Shoes?

Have you ever stopped to wonder who taught your child to tie his or her shoes? I did once. This simple question presented a herd of other more significant questions for me. Here is how what began as a simple item to ponder wound up changing my life and role as a mother of two.

It all started early one morning, as I was rushing around the house in my usual fashion trying to find coats, mittens, backpacks, school lunches, milk money, and stashed homework. Getting my kids to day care before school at the wee hour of 6 A.M. was quite an ordeal. On this particular morning, I tripped over my daughter who was bent over my son, doing who knows what!

I scolded her for blocking the path to the door, not really taking the time to see what she was doing. She looked up at me with her innocent eyes and boldly said that she was teaching her younger brother how to tie his shoes. A lumpy knot caught my throat as I kneeled to apologize and took over the project by tying my son's shoes for him. I have always felt it is quicker to just do it myself.

My daughter pointed out that he would never learn how to tie his shoes if no one taught him. He certainly would not learn if I kept doing it for him. The knot in my throat swelled until it pounded toward my heart. I knew she was right. Not only had I missed the boat on shoe tying lessons, I had been missing the boat of genuine motherhood also. My thoughts quickly shifted to my daughter and I asked, "Honey, who taught you how to tie your shoes?"

“Lee Lee,” she responded. (This is what she called her former babysitter.)

That was the clincher of the whole morning fiasco when my motivation to be a good mother was brutally challenged. The realization that I had not even taken the time to teach my children how to tie their shoes crushed my spirit to a pulp. I dropped my head in remorse and apologized silently. Then, I turned and grabbed the children by the hand to return them to the living room.

I told them I was truly sorry for all of the things I had not taught them, all the places we had not been going, all the trips to the park we had missed, and lastly, for not teaching them both how to tie their shoes. It is amazing how one simple event can symbolize so much more.

I called in sick that day, and I was truly sick—sick of work. I used up a lot of accumulated sick time and vacation time throughout the rest of that year until the day I quit to become a full-fledged mom. I figured the restaurant could do without me better than my children could. I worked with my son each morning and night until he learned from me how to tie his shoes. Although I missed teaching my daughter, we learn many other lessons in life as we experience each of our days together.

Kids do not always realize how very important they are in the lives of parents. It is up to us to show them. Parents do not always realize how much they can learn from a child if they only take the time to really listen. Maybe we can all begin a self-analysis of our parenting skills by asking one simple question, “Who taught your child to tie his shoes?”

Dandelion Dandy

Dandelion dandy, it's so much fun
to watch dandelions change under
the sun.

From plumping circles of sunshine
to summer snowflakes of white.

Dandelion, can you tell me the secret of life?
And how you evolve from a mustard color
to tiny seeds of white?

And all in the springtime to fade in the fall.
Fade into seeds that yield to a blow.
Dandelion dandy, it's time for me to go
and find other treasures hidden before the snow.

God places tiny gifts in nature's hand... the small.
Gifts for us to uncover, the dandelion merely one in all.

The Man in the Front Pew

There once was a stout, bald man. He always sat in the front pew of the church, right in front of the cross. He did not attend a fancy or glamorous church. It was plain and very simple; in fact, the cross in front was made of bamboo sticks attached together with coarse rope. When the congregation rose to sing their praises, this ragged and poor man was always the first to rise. As each song began, he would slowly lift his right hand toward the cross where he progressively spread each finger until his hand rested open above his head.

I couldn't help but wonder, as I sat toward the back of the church, what this poor, simple man found in raising his hand so high to the cross. "He must have a connection beyond that which lies in the hearts of most," I thought as I observed curiously. As Sundays passed, I continued to watch this man in amazement and admiration as he raised his right hand to the cross every time we sang.

Then, my own personal transformation came. The pages of the passing year brought about a new book in my life—a time where I, too, began to experience the Spirit. I slowly edged my way from the back of that small church closer to the front. My heart began to rejoice as I sang praises of thanksgiving. Although I had grown immensely in faith, I still watched the man in the front pew with wonder. I was beginning to long for that which he had.

One Sunday, a few years after I originally began watching the poor, bald man in rags, I found the courage to set aside my self-consciousness and raise my right hand to the cross as we were singing hymns. I will never forget how overwhelmed I was to immediately discover his secret joy. I felt a warm spot, which seemed to fill a hole that felt like it was in the center of my palm. I spread my fingers wide as the sensation of a piercing light warmed this special spot in the center of my hand.

I don't sit and wonder anymore how and why the man in the front pew of the church is connected beyond what most find in their hearts. I have discovered in my own hand that each of us has a unique and special ability to connect with the Spirit of God. His light can penetrate the souls of all. Sacrificing things in my life for Jesus and willingly bearing a cross in His name provides a "special spot in the palm of my hand" that only the light of the Spirit can fill. His warmth fills my soul, even as the man in the front pew and I lift our right hands to a simple, bamboo cross.

God's Eternal Reality

God imprints His plans in the core of life. He lifts hearts reaching toward destiny.

He is the core of the universe, the center of all matter. He lifts the spirit that centers in His love.

We can discover eternity in searching for the core within, the center of our own eternal reality.

God's love becomes the fruit of passion as we cultivate in His seeds of wisdom and comfort.

Sharing His seeds of love, we can fertilize the world in His grace, scattering seeds of the fruit.

We can join the universe in its core, bearing fruit of the earth. We can live forever in completeness.

We can participate in God's eternal reality through faithfully nesting in the core of His fruit.

We can joyfully build His heavenly kingdom in reaching beyond to scatter our seeds in love.

God's promises complete the soul; we can be one with Him and the universe. His core completes our spirit.

Pearl Earrings

Susan's children bought her a pair of 24 carat gold, polished pearl earrings one year for an anniversary gift. These were no ordinary earrings, just as her anniversary was far from the usual. You see, Susan was married three times, twice before and now for one year the third time. Through ten years and multiple relationships, this was the first time her kids gave her a gift. Somehow, seeing their mama abused in previous relationships did not set the stage for many anniversary celebrations.

They were extremely apprehensive, as most children would be in struggling through two separate divorces. After a while, they begin to wonder what purpose marriage serves but to destroy love. They know giving up on anything—especially marriage—is wrong, but they don't believe their mother was created to be a punching bag. Do they dare hope that there could be an exception to the usual rule of failure that has predominated their home?

Don't think Susan wasn't apprehensive herself. Although she had finally taken an extensive look at her patterns of choosing abusive partners, she had still been scared to death to remarry again. She even questioned her right to. Even though prayer was a major part of her life for six years now, and she had become completely content in her relationship with God alone and knew of His forgiveness, she was still plagued by the idea that somehow she was an exception to the normal laws of forgiveness. In her mind, her former mistakes, which resulted in her being physically abused and ultimately divorced, should plague her happiness forever. She was not sure at all that she deserved the joy God held for her to share with that special someone all along.

Susan and the children prayed a lot during the time of her engagement for God's will in their lives. They did not want to be hurt again. Susan went through months of counseling to make sure she was not repeating the same mistakes she had in the past. God seemed to whisper "trust me" each time they prayed. Little by little, Susan became more confident in her ability to chose a healthy mate with God's help. Thoughts that she, too, may deserve happiness slowly began to fill her heart. Her soul longed for a mate for life.

Before long, Susan, her husband, and children were a happy family for one year. He treated the kids as his own. He even encouraged Susan to become a stay-at-home mother, before the kids were grown. The guilt and shame for her previously unsuccessful relationships melted away like the snow does with the winds of spring. God's forgiving nature touched her heart deeper and deeper each day that she placed her relationship with Him first and took care of herself. This way she could be all that God wanted her to be for her family.

It was a Saturday morning in June. The kids stormed into Mom and Dad's room with excitement. They handed Susan a small, white silk box. "Happy Anniversary, Mommy!" they chanted through smiles the size of watermelons. Susan looked surprised and lifted the lid of the box. Inside sparkled genuine pearl earrings. "We spent all our allowance together to get them for you," they said. "We have been saving for two months."

At first, Susan was sadly confused. "You shouldn't have spent so much money on earrings for your mom," she said noticing the quality of the pearls. "I never pay more than a couple of dollars on earrings for myself." The kids quickly corrected her with an innocent explanation that can only come from hearts as tender as the butterfly.

"We have enjoyed you and Dad being married so much all year. We were so scared at first because we did not want our family to be hurt again. Take them, Mom; you deserve them, really."

Susan's eyes swelled warm and heavy with tears that cleansed and polished her soul of shame. After all she had put her children through, they not only forgave her, but encouraged her to celebrate success. Children have a unique talent for understanding life in a very simple way. They can see through the tangled webs we weave with awesome clarity. "I will wear these earrings every day," Susan announced proudly. "I will never take them off."

Susan is a grandmother now. Her silver hair winds curls around her ears, which are still pierced with the same pearls. The breeze brushes against her gently wrinkled face as she rests on the front porch beside her husband. Each wrinkle tells a story—some of pain, others of joy—and together they lead a path to the pearl earrings. For without each experience in her life, the good and the bad, she would not be who she is, the proud mother of two and grandmother of five. Thank God He carried both her and her children through the abusive times. Her children both chose healthy relationships when they married.

To all those who do not feel they deserve the very best, guess again. For those readers who have found that special someone who completes his or her soul, God bless. Together, hand in hand, may you skip into eternity.

A Passage for the Empty Soul

Everyone longs to give herself completely to someone, to have a deep soul relationship with another, to be loved thoroughly and exclusively. But, God says no, not until you are satisfied with living, loved by Me and have an intensely personal unique relationship with Me alone.

I love you, My child, and until you discover that only I am your satisfaction, you will not be capable of the perfect human relationship that I have planned for you. I want you to stop planning, and allow me to give you the most thrilling plan existing.... one that you couldn't imagine. I want you to have the best. Please allow me to bring it to you.

Just keep watching Me, expecting the greatest things. Keep learning and listening to the things I tell you. You must wait. Don't be anxious, don't worry, and don't look around at the things others have gotten or that I have given them. Don't look at the things you want. Just keep looking to Me, or you will miss what I want to show you.

When you are ready, I will surprise you with a love far more wonderful than any you would dream could be true. To have both of you ready at the same time...until you are both satisfied with Me and the life I have prepared for you, you won't be able to experience the love that exemplifies your relationship with Me and is thus, perfect love. I want you to see in the flesh a picture of your relationship with Me and to enjoy the everlasting union of beauty and love. I am God. Believe and be satisfied. (Unknown author)

A Sun Tea Jar

My family was in a large discount store in the town of my husband's parents. His mother had given the kids each five dollars as a final farewell gift to a fun-filled visit at their home. Our kids, as patient as they always are, decided they would like to stop along the way home to spend the money.

We pulled over at the first large store we could find, which happened to be a discount store. *At least their money will go further*, I thought to myself as our car came to a stop. We had been on a very tight budget all year, one that did not allow for any extras. I was glad the kids would have a chance to buy a little something as I had not been able to buy them anything special since I had quit my job.

While we were browsing through the aisles, my eyes fell upon a huge display of sun tea jars. They must have been overstocked, for it was drawing near mid-summer and they still had over 100 remaining. I couldn't help but catch the price advertised boldly above, "Only $2."

Although I quickly shifted my attention elsewhere, my husband noticed my attraction to the sun tea jars. He stopped and asked me if I would like one. I responded in my usual way since I gave up my job, "No thanks, honey. We can't afford it." Instead of letting it go, he insisted that I should have one. Pretending that the whole family would enjoy it, he talked me into considering the idea.

After a long moment of fighting the possibility of spending money we didn't have, I agreed to get it, but "for the family!" He smiled with a special delight and encouraged me to go over to the display and pick one out. My first reaction was to pass the decision on to him and the kids, but they all insisted that I choose the one I liked best. And so I did. I walked over to the display, skipped my eyes across each one from bottom to top and back down, until one stood out in bright and friendly colors. I reached over and said, "This one."

He picked it up and carried it until the kids had found what they were searching for, and we all found a place in the checkout line. The kids were so excited. They had each found a small toy for five dollars, and I was excited to have found a special gift for only two. I still felt somewhat torn, however, about purchasing something for myself. Ever since I left my job, I was saddened to see all of the financial sacrifices the family made. Somehow I equated my loss of income to unworthiness. This led me to never want anything just for me. I didn't think I deserved it.

I dealt with this personal dilemma by plotting ways the whole family could enjoy the sun tea jar. I thought of picnics, parties, and even camping adventures. I managed to halfway put my mind at ease before we left the store. After still pondering the many justifications for the jar, I was finally distracted by the fun and songs the family sung all the way home from the trip.

Our first week home, the sun tea jar taught me so much. To this day I am reminded of some of the important lessons about life's gifts in God's grace, some of which He revealed to me through that jar. My daughter began making sun tea every day. She would run to the kitchen first thing in the morning as the sun rose, grab two tea bags, and fill the jar with water. Then she took it to the back deck where she searched for the sunniest place. There, she set it down and dropped in the tea bags. She carefully twisted the top and turned with a smile to come back in the house and let me know the tea was sunning.

She did this every morning. Before long, my son also joined in the fun of serving his mother. This was a new experience for both of them. When Mommy worked before, they hardly had the chance to play with me, let alone fix my sun tea in the back yard. And I never tasted sun tea so good, just as I never tasted life so good. Each of those summer days brought me more comfort with the idea of being a full-time mom, and I quit worrying so much about my salary plunge.

The sun tea jar indeed developed into something for the whole family to enjoy. It helped me become more comfortable with who I am, which is an important gift that I can share with my family. And for as little as two dollars, I was shown that motherhood is a worthy occupation!

Teardrops in Heaven

A feathered sky rises high,
above our thoughts, above our cries.

It lifts our heart, when we're apart,
scattered midst the dreams we dart.

It brings us home, we're not alone,
through teardrop prisms, His will is shone.

Reflected peace, within a fleece,
on tiny pebbles at our feet.

Feathered skies, and some good byes,
but new beginnings within them lie.

Each day we face has a special place,
for our spirits in timeless space.

Where we can go, and in Him grow.
In our hearts His seeds will sow.

Until the end, we won't begin,
to understand the depths of sin.

And see God's love, a peaceful dove,
who turns her beak to rise above.

Toward feathered skies, rising high,
above our thoughts, above our cries.

Each one is known, until He takes us home.
Teardrops in heaven, His love is shone.

Purple Wild Flowers

A potato bag full of wildflower seeds for only ten dollars? Kim thought with a puzzled look as she picked up the brown bag plump full of a huge assortment of wildflower seeds of all kinds. "Enough seeds to plant a 1500 square foot flower garden," Kim read as she slowly lowered it into her shopping cart. Kim is the typical impatient type. She likes quick results. "If I am going to plant flowers I want it to be worthwhile," she decided.

Kim placed the sack of seeds in her garage until the weather warmed just a little. When the delicate spring sun held the earth in a soft glow and greened its leaves for summer, Kim prepared to plant her seeds. She began by raking up a large area in the backyard, alongside her house. It didn't seem to be 1500 square feet, but, *Who cares?* she thought. *If I plant in a smaller area, I will have a more spectacular garden.*

Kim never spent a lot of time making decisions of any kind, whether it was planting wildflowers or choosing a car. Kim, herself, was a bit of a wildflower. She was not yet 20 years old and already had a child. The only problem was she never took the time to get married. Details seemed unimportant to Kim. She simply hurried through the many choices life offers, never pausing to consider alternative actions or consequences.

She didn't even know who the father of her child was, nor was she inclined to take the time to find out. "Rebecca and I are happy with things just the way they are," she insisted when asked about her situation. And the two of them did appear happy, at least on the surface. Their townhome was quaint, decorated in mauve and chocolate teddy bears. Rebecca always smiled; Kim always seemed to keep busy. The wildflower garden was just one of many tasks on her springtime agenda.

Kim rose early the day she reserved to plant her seeds. She put the coffee on, and before it was even done, went out to the garage to fetch the bag. She never went back in for her coffee. Before you know it, she was breaking up the soil alongside their home. She hadn't checked it in several days and was discouraged to discover that the soil had hardened with the spring rains. "Chop! Chop! Chop!" her hoe went as she broke the earth with all her might.

Kim was so exhausted when she was finished tilling that she snipped open the bag of seeds with a sheer and simply dumped the bag upside down and minimally scattered the remaining seeds. She tilled them around in the soil ever so slightly, rushing the whole planting process, just as she always rushed everything. Unfortunately, this applied to all she had ever done in life.

When she was young, Kim could not wait to leave home. Her parents fought viciously, and she was usually placed in the middle of their battles. She moved out right when she turned 18. Shortly thereafter, she began seeing a boyfriend frequently. One thing led to another and before she even loved this man, she was sleeping with him, a kind of security blanket of sorts. She became pregnant, and her 19th birthday handed her motherhood.

After a few more chops of the hoe, Kim stopped and said, "Good! The garden is finished." Kim proudly rested the hoe against their chain link fence, wiped the dirt off her hands, and returned inside to finally have her coffee. "That wasn't so bad after all," she thought to herself as she relaxed with her cup of morning java.

Kim and Rebecca had a good summer that year. Kim worked as a waitress. The salary wasn't great, but the tips were enough to support the two of them. Whenever Kim was not working, either in the restaurant or at home, you could find her playing with Rebecca. Although she had spent most of her life "living on the edge," Kim seemed to be a good mother.

As the summer sun continued to shed its light on the earth, Kim's wildflower garden began to blossom. Each tender flower opened its petals to face the sun in intricately designed splendor. They were all so pretty, all except one kind of green leafy stalk that didn't seem to do anything but crowd the other flowers. Kim's random and reckless method of planting left many of the flowers trying to grow on top of each other. The dainty flowers were beautiful, but the longer Kim watched the green stalks hover over the smaller flowers, the more she realized they would have to go.

One morning the time came to deal with those ugly green stalks. Kim was drinking her coffee on the back deck, and as the morning dew danced on the tips of the flower petals underneath the reflections of the sunrise, she decided to tackle the project. She jumped up, grabbing a garbage bag in one hand and a digging utensil in the other. She knelt beside each green leafy stalk, dug it up by the roots and threw it in the bag. She was amazed how long the roots of these plants were. In the back of her mind, she couldn't help but wonder if they were actually part of her wildflower collection or just some stray weeds that blew in with the wind.

When she was finished digging them up, she threw the bag in the trash and woke Rebecca to go to the park. She tried to do a special activity with Rebecca every Saturday. It was usually going to the park in the summer, but sometimes it was driving to the lake, where they would swim, hike, or have a picnic. Kim was both mom and a dad for her daughter, and they celebrated both Mother's Day and Father's Day. As light as she made out her burdens to be, in reality, they weighed heavily on her. She desperately needed to learn to walk in peace.

When they returned from the park that day, Kim passed the trash can alongside the fence and noticed the green stalks laying limp in the bag. Something inside nudged her to try planting them in a separate pot to see what might happen. Kim was never one to follow inner nudges—unless they hurt. Her conscience not only did not guide her, she thought it got in her way. But this time, she stopped for a minute. She remembered the extra pot she had in the shed out back and the leftover potting soil. "Okay," she resolved, "I will plant these strange looking weeds in a pot and see what happens."

Grabbing the old rusty pot from the shed, she filled it with soil and made three large holes. She carefully placed each stalk in the soil and covered up the long roots. The plants were so limp, she never expected them to survive, yet for some reason she handled them with care. She surprised herself by trying this, but thought *Oh well, what the heck...*

Kim began checking on this rusty pot of ugly green stalks every day. She watered the soil and rotated them in and out of the sun. As the days went by, the plants lost their limp appearance and began growing very tall.

In fact, after a couple of weeks in the pot, the stalks approached four feet! Kim still did not realize their purpose. They did not bear flowers at all—just taller green weed-like stalks.

Then, it happened. One morning, Kim got up, started the coffee, and went out to the front porch to get the paper. She stooped over to pick it up and to her surprise, she saw on the ground beside it a purple flower petal. She picked it up in curiosity. She didn't have any wildflowers in the front yard. She stood up in surprise to discover the most beautiful wildflowers she had ever seen in her life, growing out of the rusty pot of green stalks. They had finally blossomed. It was late August, and the ugly green stalks that she had been faithfully tending finally blossomed into beautifully large purple wildflowers.

Kim stood there for the longest time. She had a hard time believing that the time she spent repotting these stalks and caring for them could have given her such an elegant reward. Anxious to share her delight, she went inside to wake Rebecca. "Come see, sweetheart. We have pretty purple flowers in front."

Rebecca loved them. She said they were magical. "Like the magic beanstalk led to the giant's castle, our giant stalk led to a bouquet of purple flowers," she giggled. Kim, too, believed they were magic. "God's magic," she responded. "For through them, He has shown me a new gift." Rebecca asked what the gift was, but Kim simply smiled as her eyes sparkled at the sight of the bright purple petals. She assured her that one day she would explain, when Rebecca was a little older.

Kim began praying again after this special miracle, something she hadn't done in a long time. She even started to bring Rebecca to church on Sunday morning. After a couple of years of slowing down and thinking more about life's greater purposes, Kim met Tom, a nice young gentleman, who fell in love with Kim and her daughter. After two years of dating that included many hours of delightful conversation, they were engaged. They shared everything together: their hopes and dreams, sorrow and joys. They even shared a love for God.

The day of their wedding arrived. Kim chose a simple antique ivory chiffon dress. Their whole wedding was designed in wholesome simplicity. Kim only insisted on one specific requirement—her bridal bouquet. "It has to be assembled in purple wildflowers," she requested. Despite other suggestions from both her mother-in-law to be and the florist who insisted that purple would clash with everything else, as she prepared to walk down the aisle of her future dreams, she proudly gripped a bouquet of purple wildflowers.

Tom knew the story behind her insistence just as he knew everything about Kim and Rebecca. He knew of the mistakes she had made and her history of acting in rash ways. He loved her for who she was, who she wanted to be, and who he knew she would become. He saw her for the beautiful mother and hard worker she was, not someone who was destined to continue making mistakes. Most importantly, he could see she held a precious love for God.

Kim began walking down the aisle to a flute minuet. She gazed at the purple petals on the ground before her, petals her daughter carefully lay to color her path. She was reminded of the purple petal she saw on her front porch before discovering her special flower miracle. Kim gazed into her bouquet of wild flowers as her steps began to sway into a gentle glide. She was so happy that she had learned through nurturing the green stalks what beauty can develop through time, patience, and love. Learning these gifts helped her find a partner for life, a friend forever, and someone to share her soul.

God's miracles never cease. The beauty He presents through nature and the lessons He shows us through life are infinite. His grace is freely available to everyone, even those who have fallen away from the Spirit. The best things we can do are watch and learn, like Kim. She listened to her inner nudge—the quiet whispers of her soul—and gave in to her inner voice in a small way. It didn't take a whole lot of commitment—just a bit of time, a little patience, and faith in something she could not yet see.

Time hands us tiny treasures every day, little events in life that, when noticed, offer us immeasurable opportunities for learning. Kim had no idea that the ugly green stalks would blossom into spectacular purple wildflowers, just as she had no desire at that time to change her lifestyle from its carefree ways. God can work magic through things as simple as flowers, if we can quiet ourselves long enough to catch a glimpse of His will. The beauty of His grace is available to everyone. He doesn't pick and chose. He befriends everyone. Kim and Rebecca are just two of His children.

After Tom and Kim were united as one, they turned to a congregation of happy friends. Tom placed his hand on top of the hand in which Kim still held the purple flowers, and Rebecca held on through the center from directly behind. They were the happiest family you could ever see. They looked as if they were created for each other. The purple flowers held them together in the center, just as God their Father would continue to hold them in the center of His love.

The Soft Sweet Song of Life

My heart sings a soft, sweet song of life.

Through the willow, I hear the faint whistling
sound of days unfolded.
Darkness once before my eyes has been
transformed in heavenly light.
Agony and grief are drowned in a sea of
resurrection.
Memories gently roll unto the shore,
no longer crumbled by the rocks.
Flower petals open their eyes to greet my
new beginning.
The breeze softly wipes the tears from my eyes.

My heart sings a soft, sweet song of life.

A Christmas Sleigh Ride

Heidi was always close to her sister Michelle. They were the only children in their dysfunctional family, and consequently, they became good friends and felt as though they were twins. They played dolls together, rode bike side by side, and even shared the deep issues of growing up in an abusive family environment. There were many days and nights when all they had was each other.

It didn't seem fair that their early days were full of disappointment and despair, yet they both had a special talent for keeping their chins up. As children, they always seemed to make the best out of their circumstances, no matter how bad they were. And they held on to each other's love. Their hearts were bonded in a very special way—a bond that encompassed an understanding of the pain they both shared.

As sisters sometimes do, they began walking the same jagged path at the onset of adolescence. They both grew up physically, but their emotional development stagnated on the "carousel of chaos" they tried to call home. Heidi was the oldest. She assumed the role of the heroine who always saved the day and everyone within it. Michelle was more of a follower—a searcher of comfort—who looked to Heidi for support. They continued to grow the only way they knew how. They both grew up fast in an attempt to escape the environment they were trapped in.

Neither sister developed a sense of self-worth. Both Heidi and Michelle suffered from extremely low self-esteem. They didn't feel like they deserved to be loved completely, never having experienced strong parental support as children. They both became involved in abusive relationships in early adulthood. Thankfully, Heidi began getting help after she experienced a particularly brutal physical beating.

Michelle continued to trail behind Heidi, yet as hard as Heidi tried to show her how to escape the cycle of abuse, she couldn't. Michelle had beautifully straight teeth when she was younger until a boyfriend relocated them. The range of abuse Michelle suffered daily took her from being constantly put down and discouraged to being thrown up against walls until she bled so bad the neighbors called the police. Heidi desperately wished she could help her sister change.

The hoped for day finally came when her sister fled from the scene of her latest abuse and drove to Heidi's house for help. She rang the doorbell and when her sister answered it, she fell sobbing into her sister's arms. Heidi spent one week with Michelle, trying to show her all she had learned through her own experiences. She urged her sister to get counseling and stay away from abusers; she even taught her sister of the power of prayer. Heidi gave her everything she had, short of her very soul.

After many long hours of consoling and advising, supporting and affirming, Heidi's sister left her house. Before leaving, she committed herself to getting help. Little did Heidi know as she watched Michelle's four wheel truck pull away from her neighborhood that this would be the last time she would see her for several months. What little courage Michelle developed during her stay was not enough to carry her through the transition of change that needed to take place in her heart.

Heidi tried to call Michelle the week she left, but received a disconnected signal on her sister's phone. This was her first twinge of alarm. The more days that passed without her receiving any word from her sister, the more alarmed she became. It wasn't long before Heidi knew in her heart that her sister may never return. Intuition told her she had returned to the abuse and was too embarrassed to contact her. The only thing left for Heidi to do was pray, and although she viewed this as a last resort, this was the best thing she could do for Michelle.

Autumn turned the summer leaves into a mirage of colors to be blown in the cold and wicked winds of winter that seemed to capture the earth in raw emotion that year. Heidi's heart was torn, not knowing the condition or well-being of her sister. The days Michelle had spent with her replayed in her head like broken records as she analyzed what more she could have said or done. Or, perhaps she said or did too much?

As Christmas approached, Heidi was in so much pain that she broke down in tears as she and her family decorated the Christmas tree. She was reaching into an oversized bag of tree ornaments when her hand rested on a decoration her sister gave her years ago. It was right after their father had died of a sudden heart attack. Her mother had finally filed for divorce after years of abuse, and Michelle was living with their father at the time he died. She had little money, but she gave Heidi a precious ornament that year for Christmas, which was all she could afford. It was a small antique scroll, charred along the edges. Inscribed on its surface were the musical notes to "Amazing Grace"—the song that was played at their father's funeral.

Tears overwhelmed Heidi as she dropped her head and sobbed, holding the scroll next to her heart. She thought things would be better if only she could let her sister know how much she loved her. If only she could tell her that no matter what she did, even if she made poor decisions, she loved her anyway just for being her sister and friend. Heidi's husband lifted her from the floor and carried her to the bedroom where he lay her on the bed in tears. He could sense her pain; he shared her sorrow.

After sobbing for a time, she fell to her knees on the floor and began praying for a miracle to touch her sister. "Please show Michelle your healing ways, Lord," she begged from the depths of her soul. A sudden comfort stroked her, and she felt at peace with the situation. Through the whispers of her heart she knew that serenity would find her someday. Until then, God would carry her through the pain.

The Christmas season was passing by rapidly that year for Heidi. She was involved in many activities and had some projects at work that were drawing to a close. She told anyone who asked that she did not want anything for Christmas that year. She felt like a Scrooge and didn't care. Christmas was not Christmas without her sister in her life. She was going to celebrate the birth of Jesus in her heart, but had no desire for the commercial rituals of the season.

Then one day she received a call. It was three days before Christmas. It was a social worker who had been involved with helping her sister in the past. She asked Heidi if she had spoken with her sister in a while. Heidi admitted she could not reach her and hoped she was still alive and well. The social worker told Heidi she was alive, but not so well. She suggested she try her number again, the one that was disconnected for months.

Heidi shuffled through all her papers after she hung up the phone, searching for her sister's old phone number. *I hope I still have it,* she thought to herself. As she flipped through all her records and files, her eyes fell upon the old number, smudged but still legible. She noticed her hand shaking as she picked up the phone to dial. It dawned on her that her sister may not want to talk to her. *If she had wanted to be a part of my life, why hadn't she contacted me in the past months?* Something inside urged Heidi to call anyway. She sensed her sister may be ashamed of failing again.

Her sister's line rang several times. Heidi chanted silently, "Love her, love her, love her. That's all you can do." Finally, her sister picked up at the other end. She sounded very sad and distraught. Heidi asked her no questions. She just told her how very much she loved her.

Heidi and her sister decided to visit right before Christmas. Michelle said she was living in a small town up north about three hours. Heidi told her she would be there the next day. A million thoughts drifted through Heidi's mind as she traveled to visit her sister. Gratitude permeated each one. No one knew it, but Heidi had had a secret Christmas wish that year—to talk to her sister. Now, not only would she get to speak to her and know she was alive, she was given the opportunity to visit her as well.

While driving to her sister's, Heidi couldn't help wondering what had happened over the past several months: if her sister had ever received counseling or help, if she was still involved in the abusive relationship, why she had shut Heidi out of her life, etc. Her thoughts settled down periodically as she gazed into the sky along the way. The horizon spoke of turning her sister's troubles over to God and so she did.

When Heidi arrived, she hugged Michelle and told her she loved her. That was it—she didn't ask questions; she didn't give any advice. Heidi handed her role of heroine to God in whose caring hand she had placed her sister months ago. Her sister suggested they take a sleigh ride after dark, and Heidi eagerly accepted. They had never taken a sleigh ride in all their years growing up together. As the two sisters sat bundled up that cold, winter evening side by side in a large horsedrawn sleigh out in the middle of the country, Michelle gazed across the barren, white countryside to find a golden moon resting at the other end. It lit their trail in shimmering highlights as moonbeams graced their path together. Just as God had always watched over them since childhood, He was still guiding them together along their journey through life.

The other people in the sleigh began to sing "Silent Night" as tears melted Heidi's frost bitten cheeks. "All is indeed calm tonight, and all will be bright." Heidi knew this deep within her heart. It took Heidi several years to come to the end of the pain she endured in abuse, and now she must let her sister come to her own end. And for that night, she could feel grateful for the opportunity to just sit by her side.

The Lord's Mercy

The beauty of the Lord can be found in the sunrise and in the sunset.

The gentleness of the Lord can be found in a field of flowers and alongside a quiet stream.

The glory of the Lord can be heard in the thunder, and the mercy of the Lord can be felt in the rain.

The power of the Lord can be seen in a windy meadow and alongside the ocean beach.

The Lord is in all that is in Him.

An Angel of Lavender and Gold

Have you ever experienced frustration while Christmas shopping? What a loaded question! Not only can I complain for hours about the traffic, crowds, congested aisles, and bombardment of advertisement, I can go on for several more hours describing the lack of consideration, uncaring attitudes, and spiritual deficiency that exists in the hearts of most people during this season. Worse yet is Christmas shopping when I am broke. Everything looks so inviting. Suddenly, I am reminded of all those beautiful things that I would love to have, but that are not in my budget.

One year, something unusual happened to change my outlook on the gift giving part of Christmas. Although I have always cherished Christmas as a time to celebrate the birth of Jesus, giving does not come naturally for me. I am Dutch and sometimes think it would be easier to give if I were born Irish. Especially when my budget is tight, I find it hard to really trust that God will meet my needs when I give freely to others. Please allow me to explain what happened…

My husband and I went shopping in a new department store in our hometown. It was elegantly designed with marble flooring and fancy chandeliers hanging from the ceiling. I thought there was no way we could afford presents in a place that appeared so expensive, but my husband saw a sign hanging in the far corner that read, "Christmas gifts—75% off." He took my hand, and together we walked to the back of the store where we discovered hundreds of gifts to chose from, all marked for a quick sale.

He asked me what gifts we had left to buy. I told him we still needed to find some sort of an angel gift for an angel grab bag we were participating in that year. We both began searching the shelves. Everything in the store was so richly designed, including the merchandise. My husband told me at these prices, I could pick something out for myself also. I reluctantly declined, remembering our tight budget that was now near completely exhausted in Christmas giving.

As I continued to search each shelf for a grab-bag gift, my eyes fell upon an elegant lavender and gold angel. She looked heavenly. Her face and hands were intricately carved in porcelain, and her dress was ruffled in a lavender butterfly chiffon. Each ruffle was tipped in a golden seam and rimmed with golden ribbons. I ran my fingers gently across her dress and then touched her delicate, porcelain face with my fingertips. I longed to buy her and take her home, but my better judgment took control. The reality of our tight budget turned my head the other way.

Now, I would love to say that I was all right with the idea of shopping for others and turning my mind away from my own desires, but I would be lying. You see, this particular year I found myself very resentful. Not only had we been managing on little income for quite some time, I had little hope for the immediate future. My husband had changed jobs over the past year to do something more enjoyable. It was wonderful to see him happier with life, but harder to keep up with the mortgage. Giving was not at the top of my agenda that Christmas.

After searching the shelves a while longer, my husband found a beautiful plaque of angels carved in the silhouette of a harp. It read "Giving brings music to the soul." It was in our price range and so we bought it for the grab bag. I wrapped it as soon as we got home and placed it with the other gifts underneath the tree. I was glad that we were finished Christmas shopping. The hardest part of the season was finally over for me.

Christmas day arrived. We traveled to my grandparents for lunch. We brought presents for our relatives along with our angel grab bag gift. When everyone was done eating, the children opened their gifts first. I must admit it was exciting to see their sparkling smiles and get hugs and kisses of appreciation. For a moment, I let go of my acerbity toward the gift giving part of this special day. And then, it happened…

It was time for the grab-bag gift exchange. I sat in a circle with all of the female relatives. We each took one wrapped gift from a bag in the center and began opening surprise gifts one by one. Each gift was an angel of some sort. I watched as my cousin, Aubrey, opened the plaque my husband and I had purchased. She smiled as she read the inscription, "Giving brings music to the soul." She said she would hang it in her college dormitory room. I must admit it felt good that she liked it. My Scrooge-like spirit was beginning to soften.

When my turn arrived, I tipped my gift upside down on my lap to remove the tape from the package. I carefully tore the wrapping to uncover a white cardboard box. I placed the box right side up and popped open the top. I saw wavy hair of porcelain brown popping through. I gently slid the contents of the box out as I slowly shook it sideways. Little by little, out came the angel of lavender and gold. She was identical to the one I had longed for in the store but couldn't buy.

I learned a lot from my experience that Christmas Day—much about the music of giving, but even more about God's miraculous way of caring for me. I was constantly reminded the whole season that giving brings music to the soul, yet all I could focus on were our financial hardships and my inability to satisfy my own wants. All the while, God continued to provide for my needs and still handed me what I wanted in the end. He showed me through the gifts of angels that my soul can sing in harmony as I give to others. I can love the world and even myself when I freely give all that I have.

Needs and wants are often confused, which might explain some of the bitterness found within the Christmas season. I have put the lavender and gold angel out year round to remind me that God will continue to meet my needs, even during times of financial and spiritual hardship. As I continue to seek His will for my future, I even find that the way He meets my needs each day of my life is turning out to be just exactly the way I truly wanted it to be all along!

Wheat Fields of Gold

Golden blades of wheat rustle gently against each other as a soft breeze sweeps its way through the peaceful meadow. Each stem of golden wheat stands alone, yet blown in the quiet breeze, together they make music.

God speaks to us through the harmony of nature. His love touches even the smallest of creation. His heart speaks through the sweet music of the whistling meadows.

His hands of grace reach down and touch our spirits as we pause to appreciate His beautiful omnipotence presented in the wonderment of nature's gifts.

His music is glorified through the harp of the giving soul.

On the Edge of Town

There once was a small, worn house on the edge of town. Surprisingly, it was situated at the far end of a very nice neighborhood, located where the large, suburban homes end and the forest begins. A road passed between the homes and the forest, which on my way to and from town took me by this barn-shaped, rotting white house that was stained in the color of moldy wood.

My daughter often spoke of a boy in her class who was very poor. He lived in a small house close by the woods. She said it was like an old farmhouse. His folks had little money and had no choice but to rent a small barn at the edge of a forest. When she first told me about them, I immediately thought of the little white dwelling on the outskirts of town. My daughter also said that the kids in her class made fun of him. She, on the other hand, befriended this child. "It's not the outsides that count, it's the insides of a person, right?" she insisted.

I was always proud of my little Ashlee Ann. No matter what situation she faced, she always followed her instincts. I would like to think she inherited her fine qualities from me, yet something tells me her gifts were handed down from her Father above. She had a special ability to love the poor, touch the untouchable, and bless those in need of kindness with her caring words.

One day, Ashlee Ann came home from school with an invitation to a birthday party. Ashlee brought it up almost immediately after dinner was served. "Mom…Dad," she said, "I have to talk to you about something very important. A boy in my class invited me to his birthday party, and I must go. You see, he is not very popular. Most kids don't like him because he is poor. He doesn't dress very nice, and he's the one who lives in the old barn at the edge of town. I might be the only one who shows up. None of the other kids say they will go. I would hate for him not to have any friends on his birthday."

Well, how could her dad or I say no after that? We simply smiled proudly at the sensitivity of our little one. "Of course you can go," I responded, even though I was still a bit nervous. "I will drive you there early so I can meet his parents first," I added. As we finished eating that evening, we reflected on the needs of our poor neighbor, and our family became aware once again of our special blessings.

The day of the birthday party arrived, and Ashlee Ann chose her finest dress to wear. At first, I almost had her change into something humbler, yet something told me her attire may be a beautiful token of her appreciation to be a guest at the party. When she was finished preparing, she grabbed the gift she had carefully wrapped for her friend, and we hopped in the car.

On the way to the edge of town, I made sure—being the overprotective mother I am—to review all the rules and reminders on "stranger danger" issues. We had rehearsed these previously with her several times, but it seemed today's unknown environment called for a brush-up course. After a few minutes, Ashlee rebelled stating, "Mom, it will be okay. Really! Just because these folks live in an old house and are poor, it doesn't make them bad people."

I respected her childhood wisdom and let it be. Sometimes I wonder if God speaks to me through some of her comments. Her innocent dialogue has compelled me more than once to reconsider my own principles. I knew deep within my own heart that people are people, some are just less fortunate than others. We are all born of the same heart; we are all children of God.

We arrived at the edge of town and made a right turn toward the old, rotting barn. The dirt road that led toward their house was bumpy and full of potholes. Our car bounced up and down as we slowly approached their yard. The closer we came, the more apparent was the disarray of their property and belongings. The yard was filled with rusty box springs, flat tires, and other objects of trash.

I decided that I had better accompany Ashlee at this particular party.

She did not disagree when I told her I would hang around, just to play it safe. I could tell she, too, was finally feeling a bit squeamish over the ordeal. We got out of the car and began walking toward the house. We saw a boy sitting on the branch of a tree we passed under, smoking a cigarette. He looked like he was an older brother, but could not have been over 13. I was glad to be accompanying my daughter to this party.

I knocked on the front door after searching for a doorbell with no success. A friendly woman answered, "Hi. I'm Joe's mom. Won't you come in?" She was a short, stout woman with stringy hair and blackish brown teeth. We carefully stepped inside and followed her. She led us through her kitchen and into the living room where a few other guests sat who all appeared to be relatives of the birthday boy. I was amazed to discover how comfortable their home was on the inside. I had expected the worst.

Ashlee and I sat down. Joe's eyes lit up when he saw that one of his classmates showed up. He quickly introduced his relatives to Ashlee with a big smile. I could tell by now that Ashlee was a bit embarrassed in her party dress. Joe's grandma and grandpa were dressed in ripped, dirty jeans. Ashlee and I were the only guests without holes in our shoes. But Joe said with sparkling eyes, "Thanks for dressing so nice for my party!"

After the introductions, Ashlee and Joe played a few games until it was time for presents. I was mollified to see the boy receive nice presents despite their apparently bad financial circumstances. Joe thanked everyone time and time again, especially Ashlee for being the only classmate who came to share his birthday with him. Then, it was time for cake.

Joe's mom served everyone a piece of cake and some ice cream as the guests visited. Even though I didn't know these people personally, they tried to make me feel at home. I think they knew why I wanted to remain with my daughter and did the best they could to make me feel welcome.

As everyone finished their cake, my eyes began wandering around the small living room where we sat. The interior paneling was peeling away from the walls in all four corners. The ceiling was stained in a blackish mold. They did not even have light fixtures in the rooms. The living room was barely lit by an antique lamp. As my eyes continued to browse across the few pieces of furniture they had, I noticed something significant that might have explained their whole unfortunate scenario. Lined along the top of a bookshelf at the edge of the room, stood several empty bottles of whiskey.

I quickly turned away, slightly ashamed that my curiosity may have unveiled a family secret. I remember hearing my daughter tell me of Joe's behavior problems in class. Perhaps his family suffers from more than financial jeopardy? Little Ashlee told her classmates when they questioned her about her friendship with Joe that, "Some people just need a friend." Maybe his parents are also in deep need of friends.

This revelation pulled me back into the conversation that was taking place around me. Suddenly, I was compelled to break from my detachment and join in with the group of relatives. I was not quite sure how I would fit in, but my instinct told me I must try. It turned out, they were all from out of town. They had come to celebrate Joe's birthday and then had to get back to jobs. Joe's folks had just moved to the edge of town in the past year and found it difficult to make friends. I could tell they weren't looking forward to their company leaving.

I befriended Joe's parents through the course of conversation that day, just as my little Ashlee Ann had befriended Joe. We talked a lot. I was amazed to find we did have some things in common. Ashlee was right. You can't always judge people by outside appearances. I made it clear they could consider us friends. They told me what a beautiful child we had in Ashlee. I had to agree.

I never asked them how they ended up living in a barn at the edge of town, nor did I ask them the reason for all of the empty whiskey bottles. I ached with a feeling that the two factors were intimately connected. Despite my uneasiness, I followed the advice that I heard from my child, "Maybe they just need a friend," and there I sat all afternoon visiting with strangers I hardly knew until they became *our* special friends.

There are many people today who live on the edge of life, whether or not they live on the edge of town, or whether or not empty whiskey bottles are stacked in their home. Many more live on the edge of their soul, with no material evidence at all to signify their disconnected state of being. Most of these folks are lonely. They suffer from a deep void that only God can fill. Some do not know of the Savior of our soul. We can bring His love into their lives. Leave it to a child to show us that the essence of His love can be found in friendship.

A Blessing for the Lonely Traveler

Lives take many paths woven together
in creation of God's miraculous world.

Choosing to travel a path of solitude,
we seek not to bother passing travelers.

Outstretched arms, we are able to give
and receive along the road we follow.

A friend journeys along the unique path of each traveler,
comforting them in their place of solitude.

Friendship not always seen paints love
in magnificent colors across the sky.

Love heard through a gentle evening breeze
softly sweeps the field,

Touching the hearts of all travelers along their treasured journeys.

Painting plans for life in the hearts of many with His tender brush.

Paths before us add beauty to His brushed inscriptions.

Never alone, even in escape of the path of spiritual destiny.

Loving hands gently guide us to the path of light.

Hands and feet of sacrifice lead from solitude,
and create embroidered paths, the tapestry of our lives.

The Number Four

My son turned seven and that year turned the page of his first dream in life—he aspired to become a basketball star. Every evening, he picked up his ball and darted out to the driveway to shoot hoops. He practiced until the ball became somewhat deflated from all the numerous dribbles and rebounds. He knew the only way to achieve any dream is to participate in it, hoping one day to become it.

Beginning in the spring, through summer's green glow, and into the fall season that slowly faded the leaves into a beautiful mirage of colors, I continued to observe his dedication and commitment to basketball. He was indeed doing all he could each day to become the basketball player that he wanted to be. I was tickled to see my son strive toward a goal at such a young age. I secretly wished my father, who was now passed away—the grandfather he never knew—could see his first grandson's dedication. My father was a real overachiever, and I saw so much of him in my son. My dad also had played basketball in his early years.

The winter of that same year, my son came home from school one day jumping up and down as he shuffled through the contents of his backpack. He began flinging his papers one by one around the kitchen, in search of the one causing all the excitement. At last, he found it, pulled it out, and yelled for me to come to the kitchen table. It was a registration form for the basketball season. "Can I play, Ma? Huh? Oh please, can I play?" he blurted.

"Of course you can, Alexander," I said with great joy. "I am so proud of all the hard work you put into your dream over the summer. Your dad and I are very pleased with your progress. I am sure you will make a good player on any team."

I signed the form that night and wrote a check for the fees. I noticed in reviewing the cost that it included an official basketball team jersey. I told him this right away, which added to his excitement. I jotted notes on the calendar outlining the team schedule as Alexander watched impatiently. "Do you think I will get my jersey the first night?" he asked. "Hopefully," I responded, as I finished mapping out his schedule.

The first evening of practice arrived. We sat down at a round table set up for the players and parents to get to know one another. After everyone was registered on the team roster, the coach bent down and lifted a large box which he set right in the middle of the round table. He knew the kids were excited to receive their official basketball jerseys.

I watched the glistening anticipation in Alexander's eyes as the coach pulled out the jerseys, one at a time, to place in the hands of each player. When Alexander's turn arrived, he quickly stretched his arms up to receive it. He couldn't wait to touch it. As the blue and white jersey reached the air, my eyes filled with tears. I noticed the number ironed on the back. It was the number four. This was my dad's favorite number. He always insisted on being the number four whether he was playing a guessing game or playing basketball himself.

My tears swelled heavier and warmer as I was brushed with the realization that my dad was proud of his first grandson. I could picture him looking down from heaven and smiling as he, too, watched Alexander embrace the number four jersey in his arms. Although my father had passed away almost ten years ago, I knew at this special moment that his heart lived on, and that in the heart of my memories of him, he was near.

I shared the significance of his number four with my son later that evening. He could feel for the first time in his life that his grandpa was with him. I told him that his grandpa played basketball when he was young also. This opened the door to a flood of questions, and now I truly felt as if I was in a position to share his grandpa's qualities with him. There had been so many years when I could not talk about my dad without breaking down in tears.

Alexander played incredibly well that wonderful basketball season. His father credited his success to the long hours of practice he spent in the driveway, but I knew that it involved much more. I saw Alex for the first time sharing a dream with his grandfather, a dream to become all that he could be. The number four on the back of his jersey reminded both of us that his grandfather could not only watch over him from heaven, but is very proud of him!

Some of us wonder what happens to our loved ones when they pass away. Sometimes the hurt and emptiness are too much to bear. I have learned through paying especially close attention to little signs that the heart does indeed live beyond our life here. Our souls can be lifted to a special place where the heart meets eternal life. Our hearts can be filled with a foretaste of this revelation right here, right now. Loved ones who have gone before us are already cheering us on!

Radiant Mercy

His loving wand stirs round and round;
painted colors reflect His ground.

Priceless promises in the sky;
climbing mercy, rising high.

Above the world His power shone,
Reminding us we're not alone.

Through the darkest trials, pain, despair;
when we turn our back, God is there.

Fear attacks what's learned in faith.
The sky's retreat, paves a special place.

Where the spirit is lifted through the wings of the soul.
Replenishing in Him, we strive toward the goal.

Sheltered eyes meet the sky with freedom born within.
Brushed inscriptions stroke the heart;forgiveness from our sin.

God's love paints radiant colors, above our finite space.
Assurance to us all, that we can win the race.

THE FACE OF A DOLL

There once was a doll named Mary Beth. She was a tall porcelain doll with a silk dress of pinned rose and ivory edged in ribbons and lace. She would stand above the rest of the dolls in any collection. Her dark brown pipe curls, held back by an ivory silk ribbon and decorated in the petals of a rose, highlighted her preciously tender face. She carried a rose silk bag, tied by ribbon to form a purse that was also lined with ivory lace.

Even though she was well attired, Mary Beth's face stood out in startling beauty. She smiled in a gentle, apricot grin that separated her peachy cheeks. Her eyes were deep brown. You could tell by looking at her that she was intense. Her face told many quiet tales; stories that brought pleasure to some and pain to others.

To some that passed by the display in which she stood, she looked unsettled. Observers said she seemed to carry an uncertain perplexity. To some, she appeared to be carrying heavy childhood burdens. Her rich, silky, lace attire seemed suffocating, and her disposition depressed. But others commented on her apparent free spirit and peacefulness. She displayed so many things to so many different people.

Mary Beth's face did not change, yet observers of her beauty noticed many dissimilar qualities, just as those same people made different decisions about the qualities in their own life. The face of a doll does not change, yet it can be interpreted in so many diverse ways. The face of life does not change either, yet it can be lived in varying mind frames and with a unique collection of strategies.

The face of a doll can reveal aspects of who we are. When we gaze into her eyes, do we see freedom and peace, or discomfort and depression? Which qualities of life have we chose to make our own? Those of love, kindness, patience, acceptance, and faith? Or, those of selfishness, doubt, insecurity, hopelessness, and self-pity? Gazing into the eyes of a doll can provide a passageway through which we can gaze into our own. A loving disposition provides a passageway through which we can gaze into the eyes of eternity.

Who Are We?

Some of us are everything to everybody, but who are we to ourselves? We adopt many personalities to suit the crowd, losing our true personality in the midst.

Some of us are locked in a dark, hidden castle held captive only to ourselves, yet we swallow the key daily in a struggle to survive.

We recklessly march through daily tasks and responsibilities, not taking the time to contemplate their necessity.

One day, a beam of light shines into this desolate castle of insecurity, awakening us from years wasted.

Peace and the hands of time help us recover our personality like a hidden treasure.

We find ourselves as we feel the tears return to our withered faces.

Our struggle to survive in modern day can become a quest to regain life in its purest form.

We can adopt new tasks and responsibilities that will help us heal and grow.

Our lives can be painful and lonely or as colorful and beautiful as the rainbow.

The key to the puzzle of who we are can be found within, through the grace of God.

Adaptation from *Hidden Castle*

China-Patterned Dishes

I was a single mom for many years. Though the ramifications of divorce left a void in my soul, my children stroked my heart daily with the precious gifts that only children can give. I was guilty, I suppose, of spoiling them and possibly even treating them like babies. After all, they were all that I had (next to God, of course).

Take for example a time when my son turned four. My friends recommended I start him in preschool. I was initially anxious. Somehow, I envisioned holding on to him tighter until he reached kindergarten age. He was born prematurely in the midst of severe turmoil in my life. Luckily, I overcame my fear and uncertainty and enrolled him in preschool that year anyway.

One day, after picking him up from school, my son delivered news of a surprise as we traveled home. He was making me a special gift for Mother's Day. "You cannot see it until it is finished," he said excitedly. It was so nice to see him happy about school. I was glad I had made the right decision with the help of friends.

Sure enough, two weeks later, he came skipping out of preschool with a package in his hand. It was flat and square. He was hugging it as if his life depended on this treasure. I met him by the front walkway with a big smile and asked, "Could this be my surprise?" Jumping up and down he replied, "Yes! I can't wait for you to open it. Do you have to wait until Mother's Day?"

On the way home, we decided I would open it that day. When we arrived,

I sat down on the couch, and he put the gift in my lap. I carefully tore the wrapping to uncover a box, which held my surprise. I lifted the lid of the box and discovered a plate. It was a piece of hard plastic dinnerware upon which he had painted the inscriptions of a memory I will cherish in my heart forever.

You see, we had been a family of three for four years at that time. I suffered in a horribly destructive marriage, which ended shortly after my son was born. The brushed paint on the plate told the story of our separated family. He had carefully designed a house at the bottom of the picture. It had blue trim, just like our home. Our house stood in separation. There was a tree on one side and a family of three on the other. He drew in brown the stick silhouettes of a mom beside her two children.

Above the house, tree, and family was of important interest. He had painted several hearts that rose up between our home and the sky, like clouds and had painted a large, golden sun in the middle of the sky at the top. Then, he had drawn a solid, light blue line, which separated the sky into two zones, above the clouds and below. Above, he repeated three of the red, heart clouds. It looked like they were holding hands in heaven.

Although it initially tore me apart to see the broken family below, the rest of his painting brought me great comfort. I saw the love the three of us shared. It seemed as if he was happy with only his mom and sister. At least our home was peaceful. I had, indeed, done the best I could to create a wholesome family life with God's help in the painful remnants of divorce.

Years later, God showed me that special someone he was preparing me to receive as a partner for life. By then, I had been eating on the same special plate my son had given me for many hundreds of meals. I refused to eat on anything else. After this man softened my attitude toward entering into another relationship, we began to date. He married our family (not just me), and the three of us became like one with him. After only a short time, it seemed as if we had never been broken at all. God indeed blessed me with another chance to be made complete.

My mom was so excited about our new family, she sent us $50 for our first Christmas together. She wrote on the card that we should spend the money on something nice for the family. Days after we received the money, my son and I were at a shopping center finalizing our list of presents to buy. Along our journey, we came across a stack of boxes that contained beautiful sets of handcrafted, china dinnerware. They were marked down to $48, just low enough that we might also afford the tax.

These dishes were so elegant, I could hardly believe the price. They were engraved in magnificently etched china colors. I was most attracted to the set that was decorated in delicate flower patterns. Each beveled piece bore the inscriptions of rosy tulips, powder blue daisies, marigolds, and lavender lilies. The $50 from my mom began burning a hole in my purse. Our old dishes were from my first marriage. They were all chipped and beaten by the hands that once passed my time.

My son and I decided to purchase the set of china dishes patterned in flowers. Our only question was how we would carry the heavy box, but together we managed, just as we always had throughout the years. We loaded them into the trunk of the car and drove home to wrap them for our families' first Christmas gift. They didn't fit under the tree, so we scooted them beside it, placing it right in front so the whole family could enjoy and anticipate opening this special gift.

Christmas Day arrived. The kids woke early as usual to open presents. "Let's open the big box first," they cried. My son knew what it was, but my daughter and husband were to be surprised. They tore the wrap until the delicate china patterned dishes appeared. Everyone was very pleased. "What a perfect gift for the whole family," my husband said. "We will all use them, every evening as we eat dinner together!" My daughter looked a bit skeptical as she always did when something or someone new was first introduced to the family.

I prepared Christmas dinner after we were done opening gifts. I unpacked and dusted each new dish as the turkey was basting. I unloaded the old dishes from the cupboards before placing the new ones inside. I paused when I reached the special plate painted by my son. I took it in my hand and lifted it slowly out of the cupboard as I faced the painted picture toward my face. Then, I lowered the plate to my heart where, for a moment, I hugged its precious design and memory. I set this special treasure to the side, apart from the other dishes on the counter.

When all the new dishes were arranged in the cupboards, I took the old dishes off the counter to package for the goodwill store near our home. Then, I took the plate my son had made and placed it on top of the china patterned plates. I still intended on using this occasionally. "At least I must keep it for memory's sake." As much as I loved the flower decorated china, my heart remained with the dish handcrafted with care by my son. It was his little way of giving me hope and comfort during a time when my heart felt so torn apart.

Dinnertime arrived. I rang the copper bell from the kitchen and everyone came running with drooling appetites. On the table (along with a scrumptious meal) was the fine china dinnerware, plus one homemade, plastic dinner plate. It was set in my spot. It bore the ever-familiar markings of a house, three brown stick people, and a sky filled with hearts. My son said, "Mom, you don't have to eat off that plate anymore. We have beautiful new dishes, and we are no longer alone. Anyway, I forgot to draw Dad by the house. Actually, I didn't even know him then."

I had to think for a minute about his thoughtful statements. Glancing at the special plate, I noticed the three hearts above the sky. I replied, "Honey, we were never alone. Look at your picture." I held it up and continued, "Our souls held hands in heaven, waiting for the special day when we knew God would bless our family with a good father. I am grateful that He has, but will always cherish the precious memories of the endless love I received from my children to see me through the lonely times. This plate will always remind me of how blessed I have been, even before Daddy became part of our family."

That was indeed the perfect beginning to the rest of our lives in happiness together. The new was wonderful, yet the old I treasured in the heart of golden memories. God indeed carried me through dark valleys in my life, partially through the gifts I received from my children. Then, as I became ready for Him to complete my soul, I was blessed to find a lifelong mate in my best friend. The china-patterned dishes show me the infinite hope God offers through His unconditional blessings; the plastic painted plate, designed especially for me by my son, shows me that every day of my life is worth cherishing.

If I Were a Tree

If I were a tree…what would my branches look like? Would each branch represent an era in my life, some good and others bad?

Some of my branches would be beautifully strong, fresh with new growth. Others may be old, withered, and bent…abused by the hands of time.

Yet, all of my branches would belong, each holding precious memories and my trunk would nourish and appreciate every one.

My branches would all have value and significance. I could use each one to become in my created image. Each would take unique curves and twists, which the hands of time turn to shape and mold my life.

Through time, the old and withered branches of my tree could grow new life and through this process, I could learn to accept my past experiences.

Each branch would represent a special memory, designed in a splendor that chases its way up toward the heavens. My beauty would come from becoming a part of myself.

A tree is content in one place, still…alone in itself. It rests in a soft breeze. Even a dark tree holds special beauty, for within her darkness she conceals secrets of life.

The tree knows of the gifts that come freely through gratitude. The tree knows of the importance of resting in God's peace.

MAMA'S KISSES HEAL ALL WOUNDS

If you have children, you know without a doubt they can sometimes be accident prone. Whether the incident happens to be falling off a bicycle, skateboard, or fence; or even tumbling while roller skating, playing tag, or stubbing a toe—children have an innate knack for hurting themselves. The hours of a day are usually fresh when the first "boo-boo" occurs, especially for toddlers.

Have you ever noticed that there is one common remedy to treat the multitude of childhood accidents? There is a generic cure-all that is guaranteed to work against tears, sadness, and disappointment. There is one ultimate treatment for the wide array of "ouches" that parents run into. It is truly amazing and proven effective time and time again.

It's Mama's kisses! That's right. Mama's kisses heal all wounds from the top of shaggy heads to the bottom of tiny toes. No matter where the location of the "owie" or how painful it may seem, Mama's kisses soften the blow. Her kisses may leave the wound in the exact same condition, but the tender touch of her loving lips makes it all feel better.

Now, come on. We all know that kisses do not physically mend torn tissue. For that matter, it does not stand to reason that kisses can affect any of the factors in the healing of abrasions such as blood coagulation, tissue replacement, or platelet distribution. So what gives?

"Mama's kisses heal the mind." The physical evidence may not support this theory; however, the psychological results of a mother's kiss on a wound are statistically earth shattering.

Nine out of ten kids when tested showed dramatic mental improvement within the first five minutes of the abrasion when their mama kissed their wound as soon as she heard their cry. The remaining 10% were affection seekers and milked the wound and kiss exchange for close to an hour. In observing direct evidence presented in my own personal experience, I support the theory that there remains a sort of "magical love remedy" in the lips (and heart) of a mother.

Thank God for mamas and their kisses. Without them, doctors' offices and outpatient emergency clinics would be even more overcrowded than they already are. To match the innate tendency of children toward recklessness, God designed mothers with hearts of gold. Try this theory out for yourself if you are skeptical. Mama's kisses heal all wounds.

Gifts From Above

A Mother

A mother's love is a gift from above. Her love is cherished forever.

Her kind words and helpful nature inspire us to grow together.

Mom lifts us up when we're feeling down,
her smile shines bright with love.

Her tender praise helps mold us; she is truly a gift from above.

A Baby

A baby is a treasure.
Another gift from above.
Needing patience and kindness
And lots and lots of love.

A baby's born in trust.
Their faithful little hands
Touch your face and stroke your heart.
Care is all that they demand.

Grace

My husband, Rick, and I had been married almost one year when we took our first "couple" vacation. Our first summer together, we decided to travel south to visit his grandparents. Sparkling in the light of being newlyweds, we began an eight-hour road trip to the small farm town where they lived. I didn't know his grandparents very well yet. I was shy, but looked forward to the trip anyway. Rick always beamed when he talked about both of them, especially his grandpa.

He and I talked quite a bit on our way down south. Rick told me story after story of the "good old days." His face was lit by a continuous glow of love and pleasant memories. The only time I saw his face dim was when he referred to the times he spent with his cousin on the farm. "We were like brothers," he said, "I was a bit older and a lot naughtier. I used to tease him until he would sometimes even cry."

My husband's only cousin tragically passed away in a car crash when he was just 18. This left Rick as the only grandchild. I am sure this contributed to his persistent need to make this long journey to visit his grandparents. And I could tell his grandpa held a very special place in his heart.

We arrived at dusk. The dark orange sun bedded herself against a velvet sky that illuminated strands of wheat, corn, and beans in an illustrious glow. I had to admit the open country was beautifully serene. The rolling land was interrupted only by an occasional windmill that slowly waved its arms in the soft evening breeze. The wind brushed across the crops as the country sky became painted in magnificent colors.

I heard his grandmother holler a cheerful greeting as the rusty hinges on their porch door swung open and slammed the door shut behind her. She pleasantly invited us to come inside. We picked up our luggage and carried it into the house behind her. We followed her through the kitchen and into the living room, where I saw his grandpa sitting in a large recliner. "Hey, boy!" he yelled. "Come over here and let me take a look at you!"

I stood in the corner of the living room and watched Rick strut over toward his grandpa. He was so tickled to see him. He leaned over the recliner to give his grandpa a hug, but he received a whisker burn instead. His grandpa laughed from the bottom of his belly as my husband pulled away with a contented smile. "You got me again, Grandpa," he said.

I wasn't quite sure about his grandpa, and I suppose that didn't matter at the time. I was shy, and he was gruff. Rick loved him very much so I would try to get along. "Honey, come on over and meet Grandpa," he shouted to me in the corner. "Grandpa, meet my beautiful wife," he said, which added to my embarrassment.

The weekend continued much the same way. They all told story after story of the "good old days," which brought many smiles and some tears. I saw every nook and cranny of their small farm town, from the open corn fields to the cemetery where Rick's cousin was laid to rest. All the while, his grandpa kept teasing me. Although he meant well, I slowly became more and more annoyed.

Finally, we reached our last day. We all sat together at their dining room table for a nice homemade meal before we left. I was still feeling awkward and out of place. I had to continually remind myself to be patient, kind, and understanding. I sensed how much the weekend meant to my husband, and he meant so very much to me. I didn't want to do or say anything that might take away from his enjoyment of the visit.

The three of us waited in our seats while his grandma brought us the rolls and butter. When she sat down, I looked at Rick inquisitively. You see, as a couple, we always prayed before eating a meal. Although he was not used to this tradition when we first met, he knew how important it was to me and soon learned to participate with me in prayer.

He quickly glanced around the table to see his grandparents helping themselves to the food already. He kind of shrugged his shoulders and gently took my hand in his. Together, we closed our eyes and said our prayers silently. I felt him squeeze my hand when we were both finished.

Then came the last straw. I had tolerated his grandpa so well all weekend, but that dinner almost made me lose my temper. After we opened our eyes, his grandpa glared at me and asked in a rude tone if I cared to share our devotions.

I shrunk in my chair as I desperately wanted to slip underneath the table. I was shy to begin with.When Rick and I had held hands silently to share our prayers, I didn't expect us to be cornered and challenged. This was indeed the final confrontation, teasing or not. Yet, I swallowed all of the anger and rage I was feeling and simply said, "No, thank you."

I remained very quiet throughout the meal. I focused on trying to be pleasant, but was determined not to reconsider on sharing our devotions. "He should lead the family in prayer at mealtime, anyway," I thought grudgingly. "He is the head of the household." Resentment continued to grip my mind as I finished dinner. Thankfully, we packed our things and headed for home shortly thereafter.

I didn't care to accompany Rick that next summer when he visited his grandparents at their small farm town. I conveniently became busy at work. "You go and have a good time, honey," I insisted. "I don't mind being home alone." I am sure he knew why I didn't care to go. Although he seemed disappointed, he also respected my feelings.

Again, before he left, I took time to listen to Rick's stories of "the good old days." I saw the old, familiar, warm glow return to his face as he packed his bags to head down south. He even picked up a slow drawl as he talked. Although I was happy to see him so highly excited, I was also relieved that I didn't have to go this time. There was something between his grandpa and me, something that didn't quite click.

When he returned from his visit, again I listened to the stories they shared. They drove through all the nooks and crannies in the small farm town from the old grain elevators to the lonely cemetery where their only other grandson lay to rest. I held Rick's hand for hours as he shared all of his wonderful experiences while he was away. "My grandma and grandpa sure wished you could have come, though," he said. I just smiled and said, "Hopefully, next time."

The pages of the season turned the heat of the summer into the crisp whisk of autumn leaves. Thanksgiving was soon approaching when we received the phone call that colors this story differently. It was late Monday evening when Rick's mom called to tell us that my husband's grandpa had an aneurysm. It was of the aortic variety, which complicated his recovery even further.

My husband, who hardly ever cried, fell to his knees in tears. I placed my hand on his shoulder and told him that we could pray together. Although I had differences in the past with his grandpa, I really meant what I said. I desperately wanted the best of God's will for his grandpa, whatever that happened to be. Rick just wanted him well. "I want him to be returned to the same old grandpa he always was," he insisted in tears.

Several months passed and his grandpa still showed no signs of improvement. April was drawing near and his grandpa had been in the hospital since November. They finally moved him into a nursing home. He lost one leg due to circulatory complications and still could not move the remaining one. His emotional stability was also slipping. He was seeping daily under a cloud of depression.

In the back of my mind, I secretly wished I had delivered grace aloud the day we were visiting in their small town. Rick and I had gone twice to the hospital to visit his grandpa in the months following his aneurysm. Each time, I set my hand on his grandpa's arm and said a prayer for God's healing touch, whatever that might be. Although it meant the world to my husband, his grandpa was incoherent. He did not know that I was praying for him.

Then, one night in April, as Rick and I were finishing dinner, his mom called and asked if we would come visit them for the weekend. They were going to try to take grandpa back home for dinner and needed Rick's help to get him in and out of the car. His grandpa's mood was so terribly shattered, he was quickly losing his will to recover. They thought perhaps if they could get him home for dinner one evening, it might pick up his spirits and give him something to look forward to again if he got well.

Rick committed us immediately to travel there. I was again a bit resentful at first. I had important events at work the next day that would now have to be cancelled. But I could sense the urgent nature of this unexpected calling, and so I agreed to come along to help. He hugged me and let me know of his genuine appreciation. I made a silent decision in his arms to shift my focus from the unexpected inconvenience to being a supportive wife.

I fell asleep in our car on the way down south that evening. I had crammed a whole month's work into the week that had just passed. Rick gently nudged me awake when we arrived in the small farm town. I helped him carry our luggage through the same rusty hinged porch door we passed through together almost two years back. We passed through the kitchen and into the living room, where the large recliner sat empty. Rick drooped his head solemnly as we passed his grandpa's favorite spot.

We rested that night. The next day, we were going to help his parents take his grandpa from the nursing home to the house for dinner and back. This was expected to be quite a chore. I snuggled up behind Rick in the big brass feather quilted bed where we lay. I stroked his back and hair. His words rang like a quiet song in my head, "I just want him to be the same old grandpa that he always was." I was determined that night to consciously open myself up to listen for God's will for my part in that weekend. I was still very uncomfortable, and still felt out of place, but this time, I was willing to try to change all that.

The rooster crowed the dawn awake from slumber as country wild flowers opened their petals to the warm mist of the morning dew. Rick's dad beckoned us awake in his usual congenial manner, and we immediately dressed and prepared to go to the nursing home. My eyes gazed across the countryside through the car window along the way. In the distance, I could see the small cemetery where Rick's cousin rested in peace.

His grandpa was sitting upright in a wheelchair when we arrived, just as he used to sit in his recliner, except without one leg and more tragically, without his will to live. Rick sat down beside him and said, "Grandpa, we're here. We love you." His grandpa looked up to see me by Rick's side. He looked at us and strained a sparkling smile. Rick asked if he remembered us visiting before. When his grandpa shook his head no, he told him that I said a prayer for him each time we visited the hospital.

After the nurses helped us pack his necessities, we loaded his grandpa in the car to bring him home for dinner. It was quite a chore. He could not support his own weight. He was also in diapers since he had lost control of his intestines. I could tell he was terribly embarrassed about his severe disability. He didn't even tease me like he used to.

We arrived at their house, and I held the rusty hinged porch door open for them to pass through. They tilted his wheelchair and pushed him into the living room. He asked if we could help him get into his large recliner. Rick and his dad managed to accomplish his request. I watched his face as he leaned back. The loathing depression that had seeped deep within the wrinkles of his face began to slowly lift. A glisten returned to his eyes as his lips creased in a soft smile.

He sat there until dinner was served. When it was ready, we all took a place around the same dining room table we had sat at almost two years back. Rick wheeled his grandpa up to his usual spot. This time, before anyone began to serve food, there was a noticeable pause. Rick gently looked at me and asked if I would say grace aloud. My heart began to pound as I remembered his grandfather scold me before for not sharing my devotions. Suddenly, I knew why God called me there that day. He showed me my small, yet beautiful part.

I took Rick by the hand and surprisingly, the whole family joined hands. We all bowed our heads together as I thanked God for bringing us together on that special day. I also thanked Him that Grandpa could be with us for dinner and asked for His continued healing upon him. Everyone said, "Amen." I saw a tear run down his grandpa's cheek when we opened our eyes.

I don't know exactly why I didn't dare share my devotions that first dinner we had with his family. I was always so shy, especially about praying in public, and his grandparents had still seemed like public to me. Although I regretted not saying grace that day many times over in my mind after his grandpa went to the hospital, God gave me another opportunity to share my devotions at a time when they were needed even more.

I am never sure what God has to show me at any given time, or what He is trying to tell me on certain occasions. I still seldom feel at home in strange places. I am not always comfortable praying for or in front of others either. Nonetheless, I spent the next years practicing the art of letting God guide my actions and words. I was shown that partially through my prayers, Rick's grandpa regained his will to live and is still alive to this day. And, God willed to return him to the same old grandpa he always was. Grace is surely a splendid gift!

Dancing With the Wind

Dancing with the wind
I never seem to fall.
Precious moments twirl in peace
I dance to the silent call.

Dancing with the wind
My soul is filled with grace.
My spirit swirls in freedom
Lifted in timeless space.

Dancing with the wind
My love knows no bound.
I reconcile myself in fate.
I step to heaven's sound.

Dancing in the wind
I face the great unknown.
Entertaining eternity
On wings, my dance is shown.

Dancing with the wind
My breath of life lives on.
Her melody and beauty
Sing for others the Song.

Dancing with the wind
My soul unfolds in light.
All my hopes and dreams
Bow before His sight.

THE GOLDEN DRESS

Kami entered her last year of college enthusiastically. She had achieved honors and academic awards every year, and she was confident that she would finish her degree at the top of the class. Due to her outstanding scholarship, she was provided the opportunity to attend on-campus interviews with top recruiting executives nationwide. She indeed felt special, which for Kami was a huge accomplishment in itself.

You see, Kami has spent the better part of her life overachieving. Deep down, she has always felt out of place—not quite good enough. She constantly tries to do better and better, and often lives on very little. Her parents were always poor, so Kami did not have many opportunities growing up. She earned several scholarships that helped her pay her own way through college.

Kami always dressed simple and plain. She wore her mousy brown hair pulled back in a thick headband. She wore little makeup, just enough to cover bits of acne that sometimes made unwanted appearances. She never spent much time on primping and proper fashion. She focused all her efforts on academic success.

Her final year of college—in conjunction with one particular on-campus interview—handed Kami the opportunity to change her humble history. She landed a management trainee position with a top marketing firm in Chicago. One would think this would be Kami's ticket to paradise. At first, it even began to change Kami's perspective on life.

After graduation, Kami's mom invited her home to pack and prepare for her relocation. The first day, she took her to the local mall to shop for a new wardrobe. Her mom even drew some cash from their limited bank account. She told Kami how proud she was of her little girl. It was always hard for Kami to let her mom do anything for her. This day would definitely be difficult. Her father, as usual, did not come along.

As they shopped, Kami kept refusing to purchase anything they saw until, exhausted, they stopped for lunch. As they ate, her mom again insisted that she was willing to buy her the clothes she needed to begin her marketing career. Kami said, “I know, Mom, and I really do appreciate it. I just can’t find anything that I really need.”

“Then find something you want,” her mom said with a smile. “Don’t think I feel good about your years growing up with next to nothing. Now you have the chance to become whoever you want to be, and I want to contribute to your new opportunity.”

As much as Kami still felt a need to refuse her mother’s support, she could sense the urgency in her mother’s voice to be part of the beginning of her new life. She always loved her mother and knew she had done her best as a parent. So, as they finished their afternoon of shopping, Kami finally began searching for something to buy.

Then, it happened. As they walked down an isle of a particularly elite store, Kami secretly fell in love with a golden dress. She was behind her mother and didn’t think she would see her run her fingers across its golden thread. She turned the garment to notice a braided diamond back. The price tag dropped down as she twisted the dress in her hands admiring its beauty. “Ouch!” she thought to herself as she quickly released it.

Her mother noticed Kami’s pause and admiration despite her attempt to conceal it. She turned around and asked, “Do you like that dress?” Kami immediately told her mother it was far too expensive. “Besides, it is too special for any occasion I will ever have.” Her mother gently differed. “You never know, Kami. You may have an elegant dinner function. For sure you will be invited on dates.”

Kami lifted the delicate garment again, rubbing the golden thread between her fingers. “I couldn’t, Mom. I’m sorry.” Her mom lifted the dress from her hands. She, too, noticed the price tag, which was now exposed. Her heart sunk as she realized it cost more than she had in her pocket. Yet, she was determined to contribute to her daughters excitement and happiness.

"I am going to buy it for you. You have no choice. Now, run along and find some new hosiery while I pay for it at the register," her mom said firmly. Kami's reluctance turned to deep inner joy and gratitude as she realized how important this was for her mom. She did as she was told, which was good. Her mom did not want her to see she did not have enough money for the dress. She was going to use her credit card at the register. Kami knew her parents only used this in case of emergency.

Her mom paid for the dress and had them put it in an impressive travel bag. She was not sure how they would pay for all of it, but was tickled that there was something she could do to participate in her daughter's success. Kami left the dress sealed in the bag so it would not collect dust during the move. It was tight in her hand as she hugged her parents goodbye and drove away toward her destiny of new beginnings.

Kami arrived at her apartment in Chicago after one day on the road. She had saved for years while working through college to afford the first and last months rent, plus deposit on a suitable place to live once she graduated. She realized when she walked in the empty room how lonely she would be without her parents. She went over to the empty closet and hung the golden dress, still sealed in the bag. She still was not sure she would ever have an occasion to wear it.

Kami slowly became accustomed to her new location and wonderful career, and eventually became comfortable in her new home. She acquired furniture for her apartment and finished purchasing her wardrobe for work. Her closet was modestly filled with three suits, a couple of simple dresses, and some sweaters and slacks. The golden dress remained at the back of the closet, sealed in the special travel bag.

Kami was successful at work, just as she was in college and throughout her life. She was promoted through the marketing channels several times until she finally reached Senior Marketing Executive. It just happened she was the youngest to ever hold this title in the company. Kami kept so busy trying to be all that she could be at work, that she didn't attend any dinners or accept any date proposals. As a result, the golden dress continued to wait patiently at the back of her closet.

One day, Kami received a memorandum. It was from the president of the company. It read, "We would like to honor you at our upcoming honors banquet for being the youngest female Senior Marketing Executive in the history of our company." Kami was so excited. The first thing that came to mind was to invite her parents. The second thing was the golden dress.

Kami called her folks as soon as she got home that evening. They were delighted to hear about the event. Her mother wondered quite often how Kami was doing in her career. She never did receive a bill for the golden dress she purchased on their credit card. Although this didn't seem right, she knew she would have remembered it as the amount was well over their usual budgeted expenses. For sure, her husband would have mentioned it! Her heart told her it might be a "God Thing."

The weekend of the honors banquet arrived. Kami's parents arrived at her apartment on schedule. "This may be the only function my dad has ever attended," Kami thought to herself nervously as she was still scurrying around trying to get ready. As usual, she had worked up until the last minute. She invited her parents to sit down in the living room while she finished preparing for the banquet. They were pleased to see how responsible with finances their daughter seemed as they looked around her modestly, yet well decorated, apartment.

After a while, Kami announced she would be coming out of her bedroom. Her parents stood up as if this were a prelude to a prom. Kami never did go to her high school prom. Her parents could not afford a nice dress, and Kami regarded it as a waste of time. As her parents' eyes lit together in the sparkling reflections of her golden dress, her mom began to cry. "I was saving this dress for a special occasion," Kami said. "I guess this is as good as any."

That night, at the honors banquet, her parents indeed became part of Kami's success. They watched through warm, heavy tears as she gallantly walked up to the podium to receive her award. Her golden dress left a trail of hope behind her, as it shimmered in the light of who she had become. Kami's eyes danced in diamond reflections as she accepted the plaque of honor. This piece of polished wood meant so much to her. It represented her value and worth. She was so pleased to receive it in front of her parents.

She spoke through her own tears as she remembered to thank her parents who encouraged her to begin her career away from home. When she returned to the table, they both took her by the hand and told her how proud they were to be her parents. Not because she was a successful marketing executive, and not because she was a beautiful and smart woman, but because she was their daughter, plain and simple at heart. Her golden dress, beaded in diamonds, could not even compare to the heart of gold that lay underneath. This was the first time Kami ever remembered receiving praise from her father and mother both. Her dad was never around much before.

The golden dress was indeed "A God Thing," just like Kami was a special gift from God. Not only had God miraculously taken care of the expense of the dress for her mother, He also was transforming her little girl into a blessing and success. Her simple upbringing was now adding depth and authenticity to her future. Kami's career polished the dull life of her parents in an incense that filled their hearts with the sweet aroma of parental pride. Kami credited them for her success. She always was very humble.

Kami hung the golden dress back in her closet after the honors banquet was over and her parents left for home. This time, however, she kept it out of the bag and hung it right in front of her other clothes. Her whole life, all she wanted—through all her achievements—was to please her parents, and that night she did. The award plaque was nice, but what felt even better was to hear the words, "We are proud of you," from both of them (especially her father) when she returned to the table.

Kami slowed down a bit at work after the honors banquet. She even found a few more occasions to wear the golden dress, this time for fun. Some of her co-workers said since she had been made the youngest Senior Marketing Executive, she lost her desire to succeed. Kami and her parents know, however, that she added a desire to live. All the plaques and awards in the country cannot give you the same joy that is found in a heart that knows it is loved. Seeing her parents happy and proud, supporting her together for the first time, brought Kami true contentment with herself.

The golden dress shown beautifully upon Kami's golden heart for years following this special time of affirmation in her life. She wore it more than she ever anticipated she would back in the days when she didn't feel she deserved anything special. She eventually married and passed the dress down to her own daughter to wear to her senior prom. She told her daughter the golden dress was from her grandma. "She wants you to know how proud both her and Grandpa are of you," Kami said with a memorable smile.

A Poet's Dream

A poet's dream is not far you see
from what we wish for...
You and me.

It lifts the mind and soothes the soul,
with splendor born in self-control.

Words sing music to the heart.
Lyrics linger...
frailties part.

A poet's dream seeps through her pen,
Her silent stories, tell again...

Hope and lessons that others may learn,
seeds of dreams yet unturned.

A poet's dream helps us find our own.
Through her golden heart...
Love is shone.

The Hockey Stick

Brent loved to walk. He especially liked to walk when he had nowhere in particular to go. Brent never did find much use for schedules. He thought agendas interfered with life, particularly the quality of life he had grown accustomed to over the years. One of Brent's favorite paths wound him aimlessly along broken sidewalks, across a few parking lots, even up and down alleys. One might guess Brent employed walking to fulfill his adventurous desires.

Brent had always been a dreamer ever since he was a kid. His mind traveled through many countries while he walked, over seas and mountains. It even transformed him occasionally into a knight in shining armor, a prince, or a famous athlete. He was always looking for that once in a lifetime chance to become famous. Although he was content with himself, he secretly wished someday he might become more.

One fresh spring day, as the bluebirds echoed in peaceful harmony to the soft whispers of a blissful breeze, Brent again began his stroll. He put on a light jacket and paused briefly on his front sidewalk to take in a breath of the enticing wind. Then, with ripened exhilaration, he placed one foot in front of the other as his mind began to wander to faraway places. He passed the first parking lot, then the second, which directly preceded the first alley. He continued to dream as the sunlight faded into shadows of tall, cobblestone buildings.

Brent began skipping over the rocks that encumbered his steps as he gleefully proceeded along the winding alley. As he was approaching a large brown dumpster, something unusual caught his eye. His thoughts shifted from outer space where single handedly he was battling extraterrestrial creatures, to what looked like a wooden stick, standing straight out of the dumpster toward the sky.

He walked over to the dumpster and reached up to grab the scuffed stick that looked like it had been well cared for at one time. Unfortunately, he was too short. His fingers came within inches of it as he stretched them up as far as he could.

Frustrated, Brent returned to his haunches where he began searching for something to stand on. There, in the corner of the alley, he found an old metal box. He carried the box over to the dumpster and set it down. He carefully stepped with one foot directly in the center. His leg wobbled as he pulled the other one up. Brent was afraid of heights—even a couple feet.

With his body now inches higher, Brent reached up slowly toward the wooden stick. He stretched until he could feel every rib in his body extend. Finally, he could touch it. He wrapped his hand tightly around it and pulled with all his might. As he pulled it out, Brent could tell right away it was the better part of a hockey stick, although it was broken in places.

Most people by now, if they would even be considering retrieving anything from a dumpster to begin with, would probably have given up and tossed it back in, since it was broken. But not Brent. He carefully set the hockey stick down and somehow hoisted himself inside the dumpster to recover the broken pieces.

He rummaged through pieces of trash until he found every broken piece of the stained wood. "Now to find a bag or something," Brent thought to himself before climbing out of the dumpster. Well, that didn't take long. It was full of trash bags. He emptied the contents of the one nearest him, and inside he carefully placed the broken pieces of the hockey stick.

Brent scooted back up and over the dumpster and onto the metal box. He put the polished wooden stick in with the rest of the pieces and skipped back home. His thoughts slowly turned to dreams of being a star hockey player, as his skips changed to skating type strides. He gripped the bag of broken pieces firmly in his right hand as his left hand swung back and forth in the passing wind.

When Brent reached home, he promptly unloaded the contents of the bag onto the kitchen table. He ran down to the garage to fetch a few tools, some sanding paper, wood polish, and bonding glue. Brent began fitting the broken pieces together with patient anticipation. Piece by piece, the wooden hockey stick became complete. Brent sanded all of the rough edges of wood as he carefully mended and crafted each piece. Then, he glued them all back in their proper places.

He could hardly wait for the glue to dry. He was so excited that he kept admiring his newly discovered treasure as it dried. He had always dreamed of becoming a hockey player as a boy—as well as a basketball player, a football star, and a rodeo champion. The timer he had set for 30 minutes finally rang. He picked up the stick and began brushing the polish along the wood grain.

After he was finished polishing its front, he gently turned the hockey stick around. It was then he discovered the most incredible part of his new treasure. At the bottom of the hockey stick, scribbled in a permanent black ink, was a signature of some sort. He lifted the stick upside down and toward his face. His mouth slowly fell open and his eyes bugged out as he realized it was the autograph of a famous Canadian hockey player. He remembered him winning a gold metal one year on television.

Brent could hardly believe it! His discovery and patient conscientiousness finally paid off. He was now the proud owner of a valuable hockey stick, autographed by a famous hockey player. Life could not get better, at least not unless he could somehow become famous for owning this priceless treasure.

What Brent failed to realize was how famous he already was, just for being himself. Hockey stick or no hockey stick, becoming a star athlete or simply taking the time to care in life, it doesn't really matter. What are most important are a person's intrinsic qualities. Brent possessed so many gifts, unnoticed by him, yet so very important to others. Brent took the time to pull the wooden stick out of a dumpster and pick up the pieces that belonged to it. He did this along the daily walk he dedicates time to each day. There are many days when Brent's shining smile and cheerful hello have brightened the hours of those he meets along his trail.

The result of Brent's caring nature was beautiful. He repaired a trashed wooden stick into a valuable keepsake, an item that once belonged to a famous person. The results of his other actions are beautiful as well. Brent walks every day because he cannot afford a car. He lives on little income. Most of what he earns goes toward the nursing home expenses of his parents. What's left usually ends up in the basket at church.

Having grown up in a broken home, Brent is used to picking up the pieces. He also understands the importance of valuing each gift God places along his path, whether it is a broken wooden stick, or a fellow traveler along his journey. Brent may spend the rest of his life dreaming as he walks about pretending to be someone important, but the truth of the matter is he is already famous in God's eyes. And what a better audience!

The Courage to Dream

So many times along life's path my dreams have seemed afar.
My heart cries deep within, "They can happen where you are."
But doubt caves in around me and I settle for the sure.
My dreams continue floating by, while sorrow I endure.
Then it happens. I feel the nudge; God's whisper through the heart.
My dreams come flowing in... on destiny I impart.
With my only plan to follow, I listen to them speak.
My journey seems so distant, my faith in it so weak.
But dreams, they have a precious way of leading to the heart.
Their beauty and direction are perfect from the start.
Dreams are placed along our path in the loving hand of God.
They guide us to our destiny; they rise above the fog.

And so I embrace each dream, and watch as it comes true.
My soul begins to sing a song of peace I never knew.
My life harbors miracles as my faith begins to grow.
And through my dreams I touch the world so others will also know.
That dreams are handed down from God, they inspire us to be...
All we can and all that we are. They make our life complete.
Planted deep within our soul, they guide us to the place
Where we will fly— truly free— our hearts in heaven's grace.
And so, I will follow dreams until the day I die.
And on the day my soul sets sail, on the wings of love I'll fly
For dreams are helping us to see eternity on earth.
Joining in God's destiny, we can all share rebirth.
Following His own heart in faith has placed me in God's will.
Acting upon His whispers has made each day a thrill.
And so I challenge all to dream or catch them floating by.
I encourage from experience. Dreams have lifted me on high.
We all have special talents that can make our dreams come true.
Our gifts become the perfect guide when we venture out anew.
Our dreams will weave together to create a wondrous end.
And along the way their treasures make each moment a special friend.

The River

When I was a young girl, blonde pony tails stained in grass and lanky as can be, I loved to visit my grandparents' small acreage. Their two storied house full of love stood tall and stout amidst a few old barns that once harbored pigs and cows. A cornfield spread its green fingers across one acre to the west, which separated their house from a river. The river wound through many fields and farms. It touched many sections of the small dwellings that grew up around its path.

The river always fascinated me as a child. Standing alongside its bank, it seemed to have neither beginning nor end. Its waters flowed continuously, yet peacefully. I used to take off through the cornfield almost immediately upon my arrival at my grandparents' to sit along the riverbank. Watching its waters flow brought comfort and an inner sense of serenity.

Rainy days were just as special by the river's edge. Although the jaunt through the field was a bit muddy, a plastic bag was all I needed to protect my rump as I sat and enjoyed the mystic beauty of the river that comes alive in drops of rain. Each drop began an endless series of ripples, which faded one by one downstream toward a destiny unknown. The river brought me peace. God filled my soul there on the bank.

As the years passed by, the pages of my life turned through times of pain and despair. My soul slowly began to fall away from the child I once was. I became distant from my heart, disassociated from my spirit, and eventually lost my soul entirely. I had no use for God for a while, or nature either for that matter. As I physically grew from a lanky young girl into my twenties, I became lost in material things, and with that my spiritual maturity shriveled. I had no room in my life for the river any longer.

The waters of my heart were now raging. I no longer reflected on ideas concerning destiny or eternity. Insecurity handed me the need to always know which direction I was headed. I could no longer follow life's peaceful flow. The river continued to gently glide along its path, joyfully winding between fields and farms, capturing a glimpse of every sunrise and sunset as it colored the open earth in a gentle stream, but now I missed all of these wonders. Ignorance stole from me my heart, which once united me with the heart of the earth.

My soul no longer followed the peaceful river either. Fear barely fed my days, and loneliness starved my nights. Love, once a part of me, now flocked from my meager existence, leaving me empty and parched. Sin ruled my life. I no longer had the courage to follow the light of faith. Perhaps I didn't even care.

But, the river of life can bring peace to anyone, even those lost in self-seeking sorrow. It flowed back into my days when I surrendered my troubles to God on my knees. I felt Him stroke my head in forgiveness as I bowed to His mercy. My soul returned as I became His child once more.

I have not had the opportunity to run through the cornfield to the river in my adulthood, although I have a feeling someday I will rekindle this childhood memory. My life, however, has become like the river. When I asked God to return in my heart, He began to gently guide me along His flowing stream of love. Each drop of the rain in my life has become part of my waters. Each tear has become my own, and they have accumulated so that I can become who God always hoped I would be...His precious child in my fullest creative potential.

I now enjoy, once again, the colors of the field. I also wait patiently for rainbows along my river's path. I have learned many things in life (most of them the hard way). One thing God has taught me is the deeper my sorrow and pain, the more joy I can anticipate in my future. Pain carves a path through my soul, by which I will one day pass to eternity. Just as the river appears to have neither beginning nor ending, my heart will go on endlessly.

As the rain touches the river in heavenly drops, today I am reminded of the miracles reflected in each one. Simply put in the story of the rainbow, the larger the drops of rain, the brighter the colors of each spectrum. Light is refracted through drops of rain (like prisms), which creates beautiful colors in the sky. My tears drop rain onto my soul. The deeper my sorrow, the larger my tear drops, the more magnificent the colors of my future joy. Light is also refracted through my spirit, like rippled prisms upon my heart; sorrow is part of my eternal destiny.

Each drop is collected in the waters of my river. The days of my life flow through me eternally, my heart knows no beginning, and I am forever without end. I can rest again, like a child, along the peaceful banks of the river of my soul. Water represents rebirth, and I have indeed been born again along my river's path. God chose me to again feel His presence. God chooses each of us. We can create a path for ourselves that is filled with His graceful waters. We can chose to become part of His loving grace.

I did not know at the time of my childhood, blonde pony tails stained in grass and lanky as can be, as I watched the river flow to a destination unknown, of the years of turmoil and sadness that were to follow. At that time in my life, I was content to rest in the tranquility of God's place for me that day. As my soul returns to the innocence it once knew, I am learning again to rest in the peace God gives me each day.

The river flows through the heart of the earth. I have an eternally flowing river in my heart, which leads me to my destiny. It winds me across fields and between dwellings; it even sometimes cuts through mountains, but it always returns me to myself. His waters replenish my soul along my path to eternity.

A Kiss of Rain

God's mercy is shed upon the earth in heavenly specks.
God gently bathes the land in His kiss of rain.
Nature drinks this kiss of love,
That falls from the sky, a gift from above.
It pierces the soil in wisdom of refreshment,
Like tears falling from heaven, rain cries our sorrow.
Yet, raindrops tell a sweet tale of tomorrow.
The beauty of God's love reflected through prisms of tranquility.
Flowers fill their cups as God sprinkles delicate agility.
Drops of rain ripple in my heart as eternity circles in my mind,
A kiss of new life that germinates earth's time.
Rain dances across memories as it lays the past to sleep.
The rainbow bows when her dance is complete.
Sunshine bids the kiss goodbye as His smile retreats to the heavens.

Pixie Sticks

Some call them pick-up sticks; I always called them pixie sticks. They are colored, plastic sticks the size of chopsticks. They come in cardboard containers with directions on the back. They are used in a game. The instructions are to assort them in a pile in the middle of the floor and then, one by one, players take turns trying to pick just one out of the pile (without moving any of the other sticks). It is a simple game of patience and agility.

It is no wonder I never enjoyed playing pixie sticks. The patient part disqualifies me from the beginning. Although I am very agile, patience is foreign to me. I have heard from some of my friends of the good things that come from patience. Of course, I must be patient to enjoy these results. It will never happen in this lifetime.

The sad part of this story concerns my daughter. She is a special treasure from heaven above. She is always telling me not to hurry or worry. She must have received a mini-counseling degree before God sent her down. She received a cardboard container of colored pixie sticks for her birthday last year. I have yet to play them with her.

She sits in the living room alone on the braided rug as she slowly, patiently tries to capture each stick without moving any of the others. I can hear her yell, "Mom, I got another one!" as I scurry around the house doing those chores on my agenda that burden most of my days. Some of my friends have accused me of being a workaholic; I think they are dreaming.

Yet, sometimes I wonder if I should try playing with her more often?

After all, I am her only parent. Her dad left us when she was a baby. He said he could not handle a family. I wish he would have came to this realization before we slept together. Part of my busyness, I guess, stems from my role as a single parent. The rest, well, I don't know. I just don't like to be in the same place too long. It makes me nervous.

Pixie sticks require patience, and it seems that children do, too. I am sure, one day, I will be able to sit with her and take my turn grabbing a colored stick. I bet there is no way I would win, as shaky as I am, but someday I plan to play with my daughter, when things are in better order. Maybe I should start with a prayer. The Bible says all things are possible with God. I'm sure this must apply to things as simple as taking the time to play pixie sticks, when you are an accused workaholic.

Perhaps my far-out friends can help teach me their secret. I am sure they were not placed along my path for fun. After all, I don't participate in fun. I have heard that God speaks through others, so maybe He is already trying to show me how to take it easy. I know my daughter would love it if I learned how to relax.

The next time she asks me to play pixie sticks, I will try, I swear. This has been really bothering me now and I have a feeling it is time to just *practice* patience and quit thinking about *developing* it. I have an idea. The next time she yells from the living room to tell me that she captured another plastic stick, I will surprise her and pop around the corner to join in the game.

That next time never came for us. My daughter was killed days later as she darted out in front of a car while crossing the street in front of our home. She never did look both ways very well. It was one of those things I thought so hard about working on with her, but never took the time.

I loved my daughter very much, despite my lack of attention and neglect. Some say workaholism is a disease. I think it is a horrible curse. Before my daughter's funeral, I paused to pick up the cardboard container of pixie sticks in her bedroom. I could hear the memory of her voice cry, "Mom, I got another one!" as I slipped the container in my coat pocket. The tears funneled down my face as my heart soaked in the shame of never playing with her.

I placed the pixie sticks in the casket, underneath her tiny arm, before they closed it at her funeral. I tied a silk ribbon around the container that read, "I love you." I just wished that I could have shown her while she was still alive. I wished from the depths of my torn soul that I could reverse the hands of time, yet time never was a friend of mine. Now, I hated time and myself even more. Some of the far-out friends I referred to earlier were there to support me. I knew, now, they were not so far-out after all.

I suppose now my daughter finally knows how much I love her, even though I never did give her much attention. I believe in heaven, where we will know all things. Perhaps this is the only way she would ever feel my love. Maybe she also understands that "funny disease" they say I have.

I guess everything happens for a reason, but something this tragic really makes me wonder. God does not make mistakes, they say, but what about the huge error He made when He created me? I was not even able to love my own child properly. The Bible says He forgives. Part of me hopes He can forgive my negligence and part of me doesn't care. Most of my heart wishes that I could just die, too. I never have cared much for life.

I wonder if there will be pixie sticks in heaven. I know that sounds silly, but I still hope to someday fulfill my intention to play the next time my daughter asks. Until then, I can take some time each day to patiently sit by her graveside. All the patience in the world will not bring her back, I know, but perhaps she can look down from heaven and see me sitting by her side. Man, I wish we could be on that rug together...I love you, sweetie. I am so sorry.

The Arms of Patience

Patience comes to those who wait.
We can reach for her. It's never too late.
She wraps her arms around the quiet and still.
Patience loves the heart that rests.
She gives to us the very best.
But, only when we're ready.
Patience fills the soul with grace.
She creates in us a beautiful place.
For when our journey's over,
Patience guides us in God's love.
Her arms are like the wings of a dove.
She wraps around the humble.
The arms of patience lift the mind.
She lets us know when it is time,
To step again toward destiny.

Pennies in a Jar

My Great Grandmother Drake is a true gem. She is the kind who savors each of life's treasures as if it were life in and of itself. She lived over 90 years in a small, white house in a small, simple town. Her face breathed contentment and her smile showed in satisfaction. Nature's gifts danced around her eyes.

Great Grandma was also a collector, not of earthly possessions as much as those special things that symbolize small bits of heaven. Her drawers were full of pictures of all the people whose paths she had crossed in her 90 plus years of life. Her cabinets were full of the trinkets and souvenirs she had acquired on her many journeys through different areas of the world. Each piece represented a life she had touched in a special way.

Great Grandpa died years before, which ended her era of travel. She continued to touch the lives of those around her in a simple, yet unequivocal way from her small, white house in her small, simple town. She maintained her home and herself mentally, physically, and most important spiritually, until she neared the age of 100. She also carried on her collection of all of the special things that, in some way, symbolize the small bits of eternity that can be discovered here on earth.

One day, time gently delivered her to the end of self-preservation. Her eyes and ears began to fail her, and it became painfully inevitable that she would have to let others care for her. The time had come for her to sell her house and move to a nursing home. She knew this would involve dispersing many of her collections, for the nursing home provided her only one small bedroom.

The family decided to auction many of her possessions so that the funds could be used to support her stay through the remainder of her time in life. She insisted that everyone leave her be for a while before the sale. She would let the family know when she was ready.

I had to wonder if she was dealing with remorse and sadness. The thought of having to leave her home was probably more than she could bear. After all, she had spent over 90 years feeding the birds in the yard, planting and pruning flowers, and gardening in the back. This must be very difficult.

Little did I know, she was preparing for a transition in life that was perfectly acceptable to her. She did have to have a say in the future of her collections, however. All of those special tiny treasures she had saved her whole life would need new homes. She could not let them go to strangers in an auction.

Among her collections were boxes of old shoes, bags of handmade dolls, packages of embroidered tea towels, jars of small tools, and trays of faded dishes. I bet she never threw anything away. She savored everything she had with a gratitude that only comes to those who are completely at one with the Spirit. Each collection represented years of her time here on earth.

Yet, she truly lived for the eternal. The box of shoes contained soles that had walked through mission grounds in Cambodia and Africa. Women suffering in middle eastern poverty hand stitched each of her dolls. They begged for someone to buy their handmade gifts, and she never refused a beggar. She embroidered the tea towels herself. The birds and flowers she handstitched on them were replicas of the many gifts she found in nature's hand. She ate from the faded dishes each night, after she thanked God for her meal and for the blessing that one day she would be reunited with my great grandpa in heaven.

When she was done planning the future of her possessions, she announced to the family that she was ready to move to the nursing home. But first, she told everyone they must meet at her home before the auction. I was excited. I had a feeling she would entrust me with some of her unique treasures.

She served hot lemon tea the evening of the family gathering. She took turns calling each family member to the middle of the circle where she handed each of us a small division of her belongings. Some might consider most of it junk, but to me it represented the bits and pieces of eternity she found here on earth. I could hardly wait for her to call my name.

She smiled brightly as she called out, "Eric!" We always did understand each other in an expressive way. She handed me several items, all significant in one respect or another, but the most intriguing collection she gave me was a jar of pennies. One would think that most would either take their pennies with them, or throw them away, but not my great grandma. Each penny symbolized a day of her life, and now she was giving me each of these days to treasure in my heart. She knew she would be in heaven soon.

I took the jar of pennies with a smile. I was grateful for her gift. Not only the gift of pennies saved through the years, but more essentially, grateful for all the lessons she had taught me in her lifetime. She showed me the value of true living. Watching her live in simplicity with an enduring willingness to help others brought about an eternal quality in my own life. She showed me how to love.

I opened the jar of pennies when I returned home. As I ran my fingers across the shiny copper, I felt a nudge to surprise her with something special, a gift of my own. I knew how much she would miss the birds when she moved to the nursing home, so I decided to use the pennies to buy her a birdhouse.

The auction passed, and her small house sold for a nice nest egg of money to supply her with enough funds to comfortably survive her remaining time in this life. She moved to the nursing home with the contentment and wisdom that this was the beginning of her end; her soul would soon go on. The wings of death slowly shadowed her as her health began deteriorating at a quicker pace.

I went to visit her at the nursing home one day with the birdhouse that I had purchased with the pennies in her jar. She was so tickled. She had missed the birds tremendously as I suspected. She asked that I hang the small, wooden house outside her window, in the tree beside her room. "That way I can watch the birds again, every day," she said with a twinkle of excitement in her failing eyes. I took some of the small tools that she had given me the evening at her home out of my pocket and did as she asked.

When I returned, I took her empty jar out of my other pocket, and placed it in the window seat. I told her that I bought the birdhouse with her jar of pennies. I told her it was time for her to relish each of her days of hard work. "I know you love the birds, Great Grandma," I said. "I thought you ought to enjoy them still."

I felt very good driving home that evening. I could picture her sitting in a rocking chair by the window, watching the birds nest in the house. I knew of her anticipation to nest in eternity with her husband. I also knew of the lonely place in her soul that could not wait to be made complete again by the One who gently keeps the soul of my great grandpa. All of the money in the world could not bring her the deepest desires of her heart, yet the pennies she had collected over the years, on this day, were bringing her a bit of peace. I was so grateful to bring this to her!

Some wonder if the soul goes on to live eternally. Others are like me. They have been blessed with special people in their family to show them that we can begin living within the eternal beauty of our soul here on earth, and yes, it indeed does goes on…and on…and on… Thank God for my great grandma.

A Penny for Tomorrow

If I had a penny for every tomorrow, how rich I would be.
For the tomorrows in my lifetime and the days I will not see.
And for all of the tomorrows that will make eternity.
How very rich I would be!

If I had a penny for every tomorrow, how happy I would be.
All the treasures to discover, in the day's sweet harmony.
And for all the special gifts, I might not ever see.
How very happy I would be!

If I had a penny for every tomorrow, how grateful I would be.
For each tomorrow's promise, I'd get down on my knees.
And thank God who gives all tomorrows.
How very grateful I would be!

Watch This, Dad!

Jessie loved to play basketball. He was the star of his team. He always scored at least half of his teams' total points, resulting in many wins. His style was smooth and graceful. The ball almost always swooshed through the net of the hoop after spinning steadily out of his fingertips.

The other boys on the team admired Jessie. They were envious of his outstanding performance, but they didn't complain. After all, winning was the object of their game. Little did they know that Jessie really didn't care either way, whether he won or lost, as long as his dad was there to watch him play.

Jessie loved half time. He could shoot hoops with the guys without worrying about who had the ball or if there would be a score. This was a time when he focused most heavily on impressing his dad, who usually worked long hours away from home. Jessie and his father did not get much time together. His dad was an important political man. He tried so hard during the hour when he had his father's complete attention to show him everything he could to make him proud.

No matter how many points Jessie scored up until half time, he always called out to his father during the interim break to say, "Watch this, Dad!" Then, he would dribble up to the hoop and lay the ball right against the backboard where it bounced through the center of the basket. He turned with a huge smile and sparkle in his eye each time to make sure his father was watching.

Half time, indeed, made Jessie the happiest boy you'd think there ever was. It wasn't the number of points he scored, nor whether his team won or lost, but that exclusive time in the middle of each game when he had his father's complete attention. This meant more to him than anything!

Jessie is crippled now. He was struck by leukemia at the age of ten. His dad is not quite sure how to handle his catastrophic disability, but he has reduced the number of hours he spends striving to conquer the political arena. He never did have an ability to relate very well with his son. Yet, he now takes time each day to sit by Jessie in his wheelchair and hold his hand.

Jessie is grateful for the half times they had together when he could still play basketball. He saw a proud sparkle in his father's eyes. This memory is enough to carry him through the years he will be crippled. He knows he will never again be able to say, "Watch this, Dad!", but knows deep in his heart his dad cares for his struggles. Like himself, he knows his dad will be happy whether or not he ever scores again in life. Although his disease seems to be a losing battle, they can enjoy the half time they have been blessed with currently…remission.

Sometimes we don't know why things happen the way they do in life, or why people behave in the ways they do, but one thing remains important—the love between a parent and a child. It is a shame that we all do not savor this relationship when it is in full blossom. Many of us are faced with making amends when it's almost too late. At least God is constantly providing us second chances to enjoy our children.

The old adage, "It's better late than never" resounds in the hearts of many. A beautiful Scripture sings in the hearts of others, "Every good and perfect gift is from above, coming down from the Father" (James 1:17). Fortunate parents already realize that the gift of a child is one of the greatest gifts of all.

When We Don't Know Why

Tragedy sadly strikes in life and we don't know why.
Some fight losing battles. Others surrender with a sigh.

We can follow in the Light. When we don't know why.
Faith will be a special friend. As we trust His silent cry.

No matter what it may be. One thing remains the same.
It is God who knows all answers. And in His love He came.

To live amongst the tragedy, the sorrow and despair.
Violent spit and evil slander could not reduce His care.

So, I remember the cross when I don't know why.
His blood shed for us helps me continue to try.

To do my very best even if I don't know why.
Enduring until the end toward heaven when I die.

A CIRCLE OF ANGELS

Gary was a banker with a missionary's heart. He finally took early retirement from the banking business to follow his soul. He became a missionary and began travelling through third-world countries to teach others the Gospel of Christ. The only support he asked his home church in Iowa for was their support in prayer. He endured all other expenses alone. He had saved a tidy nest egg for future retirement, which he now dedicated to the cross.

Gary lived the story of the "Good Samaritan." He would do anything for anyone, even if it involved endangering his own life. He did not calculate the rewards of giving; he simply gave all he had. He did not ask why he should do for God; his faith simply asked how, and he did it! God cared for Gary and protected him along his path of servitude.

On one particular mission, God blessed Gary with a shocking miracle. Gary's mission field was in a small village located two miles from a larger village. Gary had to walk each morning to the larger village to gather supplies for his daily works. It was a difficult task, yet there were many problems with thieves in this poor country; he had no other option.

As he came into the larger village for supplies, Gary noticed two men fighting. Their clothes were torn, and their skins bloody and bruised. Gary immediately ran over to break up the brawl. Taking punches himself, he finally separated the two men. One ran off, but the other man stayed.

Gary sat with the man who stayed. Even though he was also bleeding as a result of the fight, Gary sat with him and tried to share the hope that can be found in God's love and healing. The man skeptically listened as Gary took his hands to pray with him. After he was finished, he handed him a Bible from his pouch and went on to gather his supplies.

Gary began his journey back to the small village shortly after gathering more Bibles, beans and rice, and medicine. He trudged two miles back as his mind searched the beautiful sky for God's will for him that day. He did not realize that the men whom he had encountered fighting were plotting to follow him, steal the supplies he had purchased, and kill him.

He finally reached the small village, and by the edge of the wood, laid down the heavy supplies to sort and assemble packages to deliver throughout the day. The two robbers also reached the edge of the wood about the same time. They were disappointed to find Gary surrounded by several men. The two thieves counted 32 men who surrounded Gary in a complete circle as Gary knelt in the center organizing the supplies. This was far too many to attack at one time, so the thieves returned to the larger village and left Gary alone.

The next week, Gary ran into the man that he had prayed with as he was again gathering supplies in the larger village. He stopped to sit by him on a nearby bench. He saw that the man was carrying the Bible he had given him. Gary told him it was very nice to see him again. The man immediately confessed that he and the other thieves had set out to kill him the week before. He said, "We followed you along your trail until we reached the edge of the wood. When we saw that you were surrounded by 32 men, we returned. Since then I have been reading this Bible you gave me, and I must tell you I am so sorry! I have decided to begin changing my ways."

Gary was confused. He curiously replied, "I am not sure what you mean. I always stop at the edge of the wood to prepare my packages of supplies to deliver in the small village. I kneel alone to do this work. I have no helpers. There are no men who gather around me while I do my duties."

"We saw them!" the man insisted. "There were 32 men surrounding you in a complete circle. They looked like soldiers the way they hovered over you, protecting you like guards. We just assumed you brought a small army in case of emergency."

Gary paused for a moment in confusion, but then quickly dismissed this strange story as he began to talk with the man about his new-found faith and desire to change his ways. They had a wonderful visit that morning. This time when Gary prayed with the man, he closed his eyes and grasped Gary's hands tightly. He knew that he was sent from heaven.

The rest of Gary's mission was equally successful. He shared his faith in Christ with hundreds. He fed the hungry, brought Bibles to the spiritually starving village people, and gave medicine to the poor. He was their savior for one full year. Most importantly, before he left, he had taught them of the one true Savior so they could continue to grow and prosper in the small village.

When Gary arrived home in Iowa, he was quickly scheduled by his church to deliver a talk about his latest mission experiences. Gary told them of all the beautiful people and the many opportunities he had to share God's love. He also told the congregation the particularly strange story of the two men fighting. He still could not imagine why anyone would want to kill him and could not believe the bizarre reason the man told him that made them change their mind. "He told me that I was surrounded by a group of men? I worked alone in mission," Gary reported in bewilderment still.

Just then a man in the audience stood up. He asked Gary to tell them the exact day of this unusual occurrence. Gary scratched his head and said, "It was February 14, Valentine's Day. I remember because I was thinking of the ways I could show my love for Christ that day as I walked between the villages."

The man in the audience was overcome by revelation. He boldly stated, "On that particular day, we had a Valentine's Day men's prayer breakfast. When it was time to share concerns, I felt a nudge in my heart to lift up your mission overseas. Everyone who attended this fellowship joined hands and prayed for your safety and well-being."

Gary felt an electrified sensation as it became obvious to him that God had worked a miracle through their prayer. He said, "If you don't mind, could I ask everyone in the congregation to stand if you were part of the prayer breakfast on Valentine's Day?" Men stood up, one by one, and when they were all standing, Gary began to count them. There were a total of 32 men.

There was no need for any further words. The congregation realized, too, that God had performed a miracle with the help of angels. They all applauded thunderously, as the rafters of the church shook in the reality of God's awesome power. Gary knew from then on, no matter what he faced in his walk with the Lord, he would be cared for and protected completely.

Surrounded by Angels

Angels are special messengers sent from God above.
They care for and protect us; their wings extend His love.

They have surrounded me in times of fear.
Their beauty announces God is near.

Angels are unseen friends. They bridge heaven and earth.
They spread eternal magic. They can lead us to rebirth.

They have soothed my heart in times of sorrow.
Their kindness gives me hope in tomorrow.

Angels witness eternity. Their presence highlights the place
Where pain will part and hearts will heal.
The soul will fill with grace.

They have lifted me in times of pain.
The incense of their song ordains.

THE PORCH SWING

Kevin brought home a porch swing toward summer's end. The warm winds of the season had almost completed their cycle of heat, and the cooler breeze of fall was beginning her lullabies through the colored leaves. Kevin had received the swing as a family "hand-me-down." His wife, Maggie, was less than thrilled. "It looks like it was designed over a hundred years ago," she protested. "It lacks style. In fact, it is an eyesore at best!"

Kevin guaranteed Maggie he could fix it up as good as new. He was excited to begin the project. He spent one week in the garage sanding, priming, and painting. Maggie only asked, "Where are we going to put that thing when your finished? We do not even have a front porch." Kevin simply assured her that he would find a place and continued working with a smile until he was finished.

He understood his wife Maggie in a way that no one else, including her own parents, ever could. Maggie was a chronic skeptic. She was also very defensive and insecure. Kevin always had a way with people. He cared more than the average person did about others. He accepted and loved Maggie, including all of her shortcomings. He saw beautiful qualities in her that no one else could see.

When he was finished, Kevin lifted the swing and carried it out of the garage. He set it in the front yard where he began searching for a spot to hang it. Maggie was right. There was no way he could attach it to the house and they had no front porch. It would be difficult to find a place for the porch swing, but Kevin was determined they would both enjoy this gift somehow.

Just as he was almost ready to give in to defeat, Kevin heard a bird chirp overhead. He looked up into the oak tree to follow its whistling melody. As he gazed up into the huge oak, he realized he might hang the porch swing in this tree and attach the chains around a couple of its large branches. The view from underneath the tree was perfectly magnificent. The fall colored leaves danced against the clear, blue sky.

He ran to fetch the swing and his tools. He worked the rest of the afternoon up in the tree securing the chains and attaching the safety locks. The branches varied in height, so his biggest task was leveling the swing. He finally called for Maggie and asked her to come out and tell him if the swing was level, as he manipulated the chains from up in the tree.

When Maggie discovered where he was putting the porch swing, she argued. "No one hangs their porch swing from a tree!" But Kevin asked that she save her criticism until the project was complete. "I will not let you decide for sure whether or not you like it until you have sat in it for at least five minutes," he told her.

Kevin managed to finish hanging the swing despite Maggie's complaints. After she had advised him that the swing was level enough, Kevin proudly invited her, "Now, come sit down with me and let's try it out." Maggie rolled her eyes in embarrassment. One of her biggest concerns was "What will the neighbors think of a porch swing hanging from a tree?"

Kevin kept coaxing her with a proud smile. She couldn't refuse any longer. She could tell how happy he was with himself. She reluctantly stepped over and sat next to him on the swing. Kevin put his arm around her, and the soft breeze began rocking the swing gently back and forth.

"Look! We are not even pushing ourselves and the swing is moving," Maggie said with surprise. Kevin simply responded, "I know, isn't it great?" Maggie paused, still quite uncertain about the whole experience. She dropped her head back to lean against her husband's arm. It was then her eyes, for the first time, captured the beauty of the huge tree from underneath, growing up toward the bright, blue sky. It was a sight more appealing than any she had ever seen. "Wow, honey! It is beautiful under this tree," Maggie said in awe.

Kevin calmly said, "I know." He never said anything like: "See, I told you so," or "If you would only just listen to me and not complain." Kevin loved and accepted his wife along with her cynical nature. He was also in a twelve-step program, which taught him to place tolerance before bitterness. He treated Maggie with love, even when she behaved in ways that were far from lovable.

Maggie's mind chased along each branch of the old oak, as they sat together on the porch swing. The collage of leaves grew toward the sky along their many paths of sticks and bark. Her body and mind reached a state of complete peace. She was no longer even worried about what the neighbors would think of their porch swing hanging from a tree. A gentle security captured and filled her soul.

People take many paths, like the oak, but we all have an ability to grow upward. We can become as beautiful as we want to be. Kevin and Maggie are two examples of how different each of us can be. God often leads opposites together. One person's assets may help compensate for the other's weaknesses, and one's weaknesses might give perfect power to the other's strengths. Couples can complete each other's soul, in the hand of God.

And, like collages of colored leaves, we can all grow upward together. Our paths may touch and cross, and even grow apart again. Underneath the huge tapestry of interwoven paths lie great beauty. God is there. The porch swing showed Maggie for the first time in her life a mere glimpse of heaven. The gentle breeze that day in her husband's arms breathed the beauty of eternal life upon her soul. She was, for a time, one with the Spirit.

Kevin realized on this special day, that he was finally able to give Maggie all he ever wanted to give her. He first gave her his hand in marriage, and later supported her needs for comfort and security. But through all of her years of depression and anxiety, he kept trying to give her his most important gift…a taste of his relationship with God. He wanted the very best for his wife, and he knew there is only One who can bring this to her.

Now, Kevin and Maggie take time together every evening to sit on the porch swing under the stately oak tree. Maggie quit caring so much about what her neighbors think. She is so grateful her husband continued his project despite her discouragement. She knows now why he does many of the things he does, for now she does them too. Hand in hand, they enjoy the beauty of their journey towards a happy destiny!

The Breath of Life

The wind glides through my open mind.
I search the world until I find
A blessing or a spark of grace.
Each day provides a quiet place
Where I can come and write my thoughts.
Inspiration unfolds beyond my doubts.
My spirit breathes the breath of life.
My heart is lifted out of strife.

And I can share what really is.
That which lasts and He who gives.
For nothing matters more than love.
This gift is found in God above.

The Violin Man

His name was Glen. We called him the Violin Man. My daughter Rose began taking violin lessons the year of her ninth birthday. I was very apprehensive. She had never shown commitment to anything before, and I didn't know why this would be any different. I shopped carefully to compare prices on violin rentals. I didn't dare buy one in case she would change her mind and quit playing, like she had done with other instruments in the past.

My cost comparison led me to Glen, the Violin Man. He offered the cheapest rates. He ran an instrument business out of his home so I thought it was worth giving him a try. After drilling my daughter about her intention to practice one last time, we scheduled an appointment with Glen to rent a violin.

His house was on the other end of town. My daughter chattered the whole drive to his home. "I hope we can find it," she said. I was just hoping she would maintain this enthusiasm throughout the year. About five miles later, I took the last right turn which placed us on his street. I slowed the car as we began searching for his address. "There it is!" Rose yelled.

As we drove in the driveway, our eyes together wandered across his overgrown yard. His lawn looked more like a field than grass. The bushes protruded in scattered directions and his honeysuckle and creeping ivy almost completely hid the siding of his house from visibility. We thought we had the wrong address and the house we were looking at was perhaps deserted.

I double-checked the numbers I had written on my notepad. "14563

Grant Ave—this must be it," I said. We hopped out of the car and walked up to the front door step. I pushed the doorbell, but didn't hear any sound. As a last resort, I knocked loudly on the door.

Just as we were about to walk away, a man opened the door. He was tall and lanky with an overgrown mustache. "You must be Rose," he said as he invited us in. He acted like he had known her forever. "I have been excited about your coming. My name is Glen, but you can just call me the Violin Man. Let me show you all of my instruments so you can choose the one you like best."

Rose looked at me inquisitively. I returned a look of reassurance, so she followed the man into his home while I was close behind. I glanced in the open rooms that we passed. It was amazing how much stuff this man had packed in his house. He had every instrument here from gigantic cellos to small flutes. Almost every instrument was out of its case. Everything seemed so disorganized.

The man must have noticed me snooping. He turned to tell me that he mends broken instruments as well as rents them to children. "I even teach music lessons," he said in an invigorating tone. "I love music and I love kids! I was never married, so I never had any of my own. You might say music and instruments help keep me company."

We all entered a large family room, where he invited us to sit down. He brought several violins into the room and set them on the floor in front of Rose. "I pick that one," Rose declared after spending a few minutes comparing their polished splendor. The Violin Man told her she made a wonderful choice. "And now for a case," he said.

He walked out to the other room again, returning the instruments she did not chose. He reentered with a case under his arm. He said, "I'll tell you what. You seem like a very special girl, so I found you my nicest violin case. It is lined in a rose colored velvet, as beautiful as your name. I have a feeling you will do well!"

He opened the case and sure enough, it was bedded in plush velour rose lining. He handed it to Rose and said, "A special case for a special girl. I won't even charge your mommy extra." Rose smiled as she admired the case like a treasure. She picked up the violin and gently set it in the case.

This was our first experience with the Violin Man. He invited us to stop by and visit any time. He also offered to give Rose a free lesson. He was unusually friendly and treated us like part of his family. He possessed a unique sense of caring that I couldn't put my finger on. He was definitely nicer than any piano instructor that I ever had while growing up.

As the fall leaves were swept away and exposed the tree limbs in frigid winter white, Rose continued to practice her violin. I was amazed at how she stuck with it as long as she did. Rose bypassed the squeaky phase, catching on right away. She obviously had special talent for the violin. Her notes glided in beautiful harmony. She had an ear for music.

I forgot about the Violin Man as well as his offer for a free lesson. Rose talked about him frequently, remembering him each time she showed her friends her plush, velvet case. His kind nature and caring ways became a sweet memory for us. I really had no intention of keeping in touch. I guess somewhere in my busy mind, I decided he may just act like he really cares for kids. "After all, he has a business to run."

Then, one day the Violin Man called. It was late January and he hadn't heard from us, except for our monthly rental payments, since our visit in September. "How is Rose doing?" he asked. I was stunned. He must have a gigantic follow-up list or some huge calendar with notes marked that remind him to check in with kids he has rented to. But as the conversation continued, that didn't seem to be the case. He said that Rose was on his mind, and he was wondering if she would still like the free lesson.

"I don't believe so," I said. "She is doing quite well with her instructor at school. In fact, she is still enjoying practicing."

"I had a feeling she would do well," responded the Violin Man.

I had to wonder how he could see this natural ability in my child, when all I could do is focus on my fear of renting an instrument and her immediately dropping out of lessons. Again, I contemplated Glen's special gifts. Not only did he have a gift for music, he also knew how to make music through his kind actions. He had a special ability to listen to the hearts of children.

"Well, at least feel free to visit whenever you would like," he said at the end of our conversation. "I would love to see Rose again."

I told him we would, even though I had no intention of taking him up on his thoughtful offer. My mind still had reservations about his true intentions. Perhaps he would try to sell us a more expensive instrument? What I failed to realize was that Glen really did care for my Rose. He genuinely wanted to help her succeed.

Later, I told Rose that the Violin Man called to see how she was doing. Her face lit up and a smile skipped across her face. "Can I call him back?" she asked.

"Of course," I said reluctantly and handed her his telephone number. She immediately dialed as she bounced in her seat waiting for him to answer the line. When he answered, Rose excitedly began chattering about all of her progress over the past months. They must have talked an hour.

When she finally hung up, I couldn't resist asking her some questions. I still could not understand the connection they seemed to have with one another. After all, he was a stranger. I had to ask why she felt so comfortable sharing with him. Rose told me in her simple answer, the answers to many of the questions that had been plaguing my mind since the beginning of her violin experience.

She said, "I could tell you weren't very excited about me playing the violin, Mommy. It felt so nice when the Violin Man told me how special I was and gave me his best violin case. He told me that I would do well. I guess that is why I stick with it. He sees musical talent in me, and I don't want to let him down. He cares."

Suddenly, I felt as small as a dot on an amoebae. It is no wonder Rose never stuck with anything before this. I never encouraged her. I always questioned her intentions and never gave her the benefit of the doubt. Now, she was performing beautifully because of the caring encouragement of a stranger. I realized then that Glen was not a stranger at all, but a special friend who goes by the humble name, The Violin Man.

The Dance of the Violin

My spirit dances to the violin.
It glides me up and down again.
My mind is silenced to its voice.
It brings to me a simple choice.

To hold the world within my heart.
To treasure life or stay apart.
The violin bows a gentle peace.
It sounds God's love upon a fleece.

We can join hands in the graceful dance.
In perfect rhythm; nothing to chance.
Gliding upon the wings of our soul,
Awaiting the day destiny is made whole.

The Wren House

My grandfather gave me a wren house one spring. He was a craftsman in retirement. He found great joy in building creations out of wood for others. Everything he constructed had a specific purpose and served a unique function. He was also set in his ways, and this characteristic dominated his wood works.

When he first handed me the wren house, I looked to find the hole. "It is very small," I said in a questioning tone. I didn't question my grandfather much. It never seemed to settle very well. Usually my challenges wound up disregarded, and later we pretended they were never mentioned at all. This was our pattern.

He explained, "The hole must be small. That way the only bird that can fit into the house is a wren. That's why it's called a wren house," he explained. After trying to talk him into drilling the hole larger, I asked him to hang it in the tree with the pink spring blossoms. Again, we pretended that nothing else was ever mentioned.

Springs came and her petals faded into summers. All the while, I waited each fresh season for a wren to use the house my grandfather built. I was disappointed every time the pink blossoms fell to discover there would be no wren again that year. I asked him periodically if he would reconsider drilling the hole larger so the other birds could use the house, but he disregarded all of my requests. "Just wait! A wren will come."

A wren never did come. I became confident one year that it was time for all the birds to enjoy the wren house. I also began to realize that perhaps my grandfather was not always right about everything. So, I took the house down and borrowed the neighbors drill to make the hole larger.

What a blessing! The wren house did not even stay empty for one day. Two fluffy tan and brown birds began building a nest within their new home right away. I watched them stand on the branch beside the wren house, one next to the hole and the other further away. The male was handing brush to the female bird who took it in her tiny beak and pecked it through the hole I had enlarged.

As I curiously watched them, my heart filled with a deep sense of inner peace. I had acted upon my own instincts and created a larger opening in the wren house so that other birds could enjoy it. I had a feeling my neighborhood must not attract wrens. It was refreshing to act upon my instincts, rather than waiting another year with no feathered visitors like my grandpa kept telling me to do.

In a way, I guess I was also creating a larger opening in my life. I had spent years doing exactly what others expected me to do, not considering the thought of doing anything that might please me. Now, I could enjoy the wren house, seeing it filled with birds. I was also enjoying my life so much more. My days had been empty for some time, but since I began doing things that were important to me, despite what others said, my days were filled now with the many gifts that come to those who follow their soul.

Thank God for the blessing I found in my wren house. It reminds me every day, "To thy own self be true."

Authenticity

Authenticity is being all that I am.
Expressing myself freely and
Knowing I can.
Having confidence in the One who is the Great I Am!

Authenticity is living fully each day.
Contributing to life and
Remembering to pray.
Accepting each event in life that comes my way.

Authenticity comes to those
Whose hearts are based in love.
It enriches us who freely give
God's treasures from above.
Like patience, understanding, tolerance, and love.

Give Us This Day Our Daily Bread

Surrendering to service is not an easy choice. It is not a thought taken lightly by most. I know I resisted my calling for years. There may be some out there who follow the Light the first time it is seen. My hat goes off to them! There may be others who enjoy the vow of poverty and humility that comes with complete servitude. Blessed are the meek in spirit!

For many that dare entertain the possibility of stepping into God's complete will for their life, fear is the first reaction that might "slap them upside the head." I know fear showed up each time I considered listening to and following the whispers of my soul. Not only did it capture my mind, it showed up wearing boxing gloves, attempting to beat some common sense into me!

Thankfully, I had learned by this time that the opposite of fear is faith. With faith in my hands, I had no need to fight. Fear became transparent. It simply disappeared! Faith became my shield of armor as I suddenly gained more courage to explore the unknown possibilities of inviting God to completely rule my life. I asked him finally to be my principle. I told Him, "I will be Your agent."

Of course, I had some major concerns jumping in front of me, constantly beckoning my attention. "Who will take care of me if I surrender my financial position to do that which God wants me to do? It doesn't seem to pay as well." "Will I still have enough money for groceries?" "For that matter, how will I put my kids through college?"

Each time my mind was captured in worry about my future, the One answer to all my questions poured upon me from above—"God." Scripture came rushing into my head to sooth my uncertainty. "Seek first the kingdom of God and His righteousness and all else will be granted unto you." I was also reminded of an important part of the Lord's Prayer, "Give us this day our daily bread."

I guess I always read Scripture and prayed, but I never thought much about asking God for bread; or for that matter, how I could apply Scripture to my everyday life. Thankfully, in this country, most of us are blessed with enough food for our days. But, when you give up a lifestyle you are very comfortable and familiar with to enter into the unknown of complete servitude with no expectations or self-willed plans, things change in a big way! You cannot plan on anything, including food. Everything you receive becomes a gift.

This might sound like a major drag to some, but I'm here to tell you that there is no better way to live. To stay in touch with the true meaning of life is to touch eternity. We can bring beauty to the earth. We can welcome freedom and joy into our hearts. I also discovered that my needs are cared for along my journey with the Lord as my shepherd.

My family has not been without food one day yet. In fact, ironically as it may seem, I received a bread maker as a gift shortly after I dedicated my life to the cross. Not only do we receive each day our daily bread, I can now prepare a scrumptious loaf that sends a deeply satisfying aroma through our home. God has a way of caring for my family and me. Although it might not always be in the way I expect, He never fails to care for me in a way that endures. He always gives me what I truly need, blessing me sometimes even by not granting me all of my wants.

The thought of returning to my old way of life creeps up occasionally, especially when I think of that shiny red sportscar I used to drive, or going out to eat at a restaurant on the weekends, or even just shopping whenever I felt like it. But my soul whispers, "Look what you have in its place." When I open my eyes, I see the love God gives me freely each day, a deep passion for my beautiful life, deep gratitude for the simple, yet abundant gifts, and an ability to truly love myself and be satisfied.

God has placed eternity in the palm of my open hand. He has shown me what many do not see. He has not only given my family each day our daily bread, he has fed me a taste of heaven on earth.

If your fear still wears boxing gloves, join my hand in faith. If worldly concerns still trip you up, hop on the wings of your soul and fly above your insecurity. If you do not think you have the courage, think again! Just because you're afraid, doesn't mean you don't have courage. Courage is doing what's in your heart, despite your fear. I have learned through my experience serving God that faith is not asking why. Faith is asking how and then just doing it!

The Cross in the Tree

I've always liked to write, through the window of my dreams.
An interest born within my soul, so delicate it seems.
One day, I captured courage, and opened up my heart.
I wanted to write my book of life, but didn't know where to start.
A prayer began my journey into this great unknown.
I opened my mind, and His seeds of love were sown.
I hoped to get my message out, when all was said and done.
I wanted to share my life, my pages weren't for fun.
A prayer began another path, eternal from the start.
My book reached another soul, with freedom in his heart.
He read my words and found them dear, a blessing in disguise.
He seemed to have an open mind, his words carried wise.
We joined in the love of Christ, to reach the world around.
Despite exasperation, my feet continued breaking ground.
And then, one day, God touched me, as I asked Him for a fleece.
His images fit together, with every tiny piece.
The business of my publisher, imprints evergreen and pine.
I knew from the beginning, this was a special sign.
You see, my home is planted in a wood of evergreen.
I've always loved them very much, their meaning yet unseen.
One day, I happened by a very special one.
I'd walked by several times, yet never in the sun.
We'd trimmed the branches up, only days ago.
The tree was drifting crooked, hanging very low.
This pine gave me the fleece, I'd waited so long to see.
As I strolled beside its trunk, a cross came to me.
I had to do a double take, it seemed it wasn't true.
Sure enough, the cross was there, etched in bark like new.
I had to back across the yard to see if it disappeared.
But through the pines it shone, glorified by nature's mirror.
I've known the tree is special, but imagined nothing close.
The miracles some represent are what I love the most.
And so I keep on writing, and waiting for the day.
When Jesus comes to greet me, and take my soul away.
He's shown me through my days on earth, eternity is mine.
He's blessed me in creation, and through His love I shine.

Magic Bear

Alex suffered from chronic asthma attacks. His parents both worked full time and did the best they could to try to manage his condition, but it wasn't easy. At least twice a year he wound up in the emergency room of the hospital. Top pulmonary specialists tested him for allergies when he was two. They even had him complete numerous batteries of pulmonary function tests and forcefully exhale regularly into a peak flow monitor to measure his lung capacity. No matter how hard they tried, it never seemed to be enough to control his disease.

One spring, the mad cycle of chaos, which had plagued Alex with near death experiences from the time he was a baby, finally ended. He fell asleep one evening feeling fine, but awoke in the middle of the night gasping for air. His mom, Cheryl, tried to revive him in the normal manner, but this time nothing was working. She threw his head back in an attempt to open his airway, but darkened blue surrounded his eyes as his body fell limp in her arms.

Cheryl yelled to Alex's dad to call the emergency number. Then, she did something she had never tried before. She fell to her knees as she held her limp child and prayed for a miracle of healing. Cheryl grew up in an agnostic home, where prayer was foreign. She had no idea how to even begin, yet her soul knew it was her only hope. The tears rolled down her worried face onto her son's cheek as she prayed. It seemed the ambulance was taking forever.

Finally, after she began screaming with all her heart for God to bring her son back, Alex opened his eyes and gasped for air. She could see the terror in his dilated pupils as he struggled for air. Cheryl stroked his forehead and told him it would be all right. She had no idea at the time why she said what she did. She thought her son would die. This, she thought, might be his final emergency.

The paramedics finally arrived at the scene. He had been struggling for oxygen by that time for 15 minutes. The only thing sustaining him was his mother and God through her prayers. Two men quickly entered his bedroom and immediately covered his face with a plastic mask of emergency epinephrine. They followed this with aerosol treatments to stabilize him enough to carry him on the stretcher to the ambulance.

Cheryl held Alex's small hand as she walked beside the stretcher. She wanted to ride along with him in the ambulance. She was still crying uncontrollably for she knew she had almost lost her son. Her heart repeated softly over and over that something needed to change. Losing her son would rip her soul apart. Cheryl continued to pray.

Alex began improving considerably in the ambulance on the way to the hospital. A thoughtful paramedic gave him a large, fluffy brown teddy bear. He held onto the bear with his life; he clung to it like a scared child who had been beaten. He continued to hold the bear next to him as they carried him into the hospital for further evaluation.

This is when the miracle began to really settle upon them. By the time he was assigned a hospital room, he had completely recovered. His oxygen levels had returned to 98% saturation, and he no longer had carbon dioxide congestion. The admitting doctor could not even believe he was brought in by ambulance. Cheryl could tell that he thought she had perhaps overreacted.

Alex still held his bear tight as he said thank you to the departing paramedic. The man told him he could keep it for good luck. They dismissed Alex that night as completely healthy. Alex decided on the way home to name the bear "Magic Bear." He said the bear must be magic because it saved his life.

All of a sudden, Cheryl was filled with an understanding of the real magic that saved her son's life. With all of the commotion, she almost forgot that she prayed for God to heal him and He did. Cheryl found it within herself to say, "Magic Bear is a special friend who kept you company when you were scared, but Mama said a prayer to God as I held you in my arms in the bedroom. God saved your life!"

Alex still swears to this day it was Magic Bear who saved him and that's all right. His mom reminds him of the magic of God and the miracles of His works. She also realizes that her role as a mother is more important than managing the home and working full time besides. She quit her job shortly after the last emergency with her son. This gave her the time she needed to research his disease and learn ways she could be more proactive in treating him. It also gives her the chance to love him around the clock, which is something all children long for.

Alex has been attack free for well over a year. Magic Bear still sits in a special corner of his room. Cheryl prays regularly now, and the family has started going to church. She is so thankful for the magic God has worked in her life through the loving touch of His miracle.

The Harp of My Soul

My soul plays a precious harp. My spirit waltzes its tune.
The rhythm sways and guides me. My King is coming soon!

As my fingers stroke each passing chord, the fiber of my bone.
My soul hums abidance. My Eternal is enthroned.

My soul sings of miracles, God's magic works of fate.
My harp echoes beauty as I play it for His sake.

My soul joins the symphony, helping orchestrate each day.
Strangers become special friends. My troubles go away.

The Precious Harp will be my guide as I listen to my soul.
His wondrous love breathes through me. His song makes me whole.

Precious Spirit

I had an opportunity recently to pray with a young woman who is struggling with addiction and brokenheartedness. I visited with her on the phone for almost an hour. It seemed she had no idea how she would ever break free of her tragic pattern of drug abuse. I suggested there is One who can free her from the bondage of her troubles. "That One is God, and we all know deep within our hearts how to pray," I advised.

I was always a bit short with people when they called for help. It wasn't that I didn't care, rather I worked on projects regularly. I always seemed to be in the middle of at least three at a time. I was working in the Spirit, so I thought it must be all right. I sometimes failed to realize the importance of putting aside my work to really touch and heal the heart of another's need.

The young woman asked if I would help her pray on the phone. At first, I felt a tweak of hesitance, yet I closed my eyes and felt the voice of my soul lifted toward the sky. Words of wisdom entered my mind as I expectantly asked God to heal her. "Jesus, please enter her heart and grant her relief from her addiction."

My skin broke out in small bumps that made my arm hairs stand on end as I said, "Amen." She responded in utter amazement. "I could feel your presence. You have such a precious spirit!" I told her it was not my presence she felt, but that of whom we were calling upon…Jesus, the Savior of all who need healing.

I resumed my business as soon as we hung up the phone. As I continued my project, her awe-struck words echoed in the rafters of my mind. "You have such a precious spirit!" I never thought of my spirit as being precious before. I know I give all I've got, but sometimes it doesn't seem to be much, especially when it comes to taking time out to minister to another.

Just then, it dawned on me what spirit she actually heard and felt, for it wasn't my spirit as she thought. It was the Spirit of Jesus. He is the precious Spirit. He penetrated through me like a vessel with His healing power and love. I had been wearing a W.W.J.D. bracelet for months. It had been rattling back and forth day after day as I religiously worked on my projects. I was very happy that day to know that it was finally put to good use!

WWJD

What Would Jesus Do?

Some struggle their way through life not knowing how to live.
Others search for answers, but their questions do not give.

When we wonder why we feel so bad?
Just think of Jesus and all He had…

He possessed so little,
yet carried the world in the palms of His hands.

Some wonder what to do when bad situations arise.
Many of us shun away; our hearts we compromise.

Just think of Jesus and all He did.
His precious words are wise.

We possess so much when we carry His message to all the lands.

A Man Delivering Papers

There once was a man who delivered papers. It was hard to say if he did it for extra money, or simply enough income to get by. He was a gruff looking man who let his hair grow in long, greasy strands. The only part of his face you could see were the rough whiskers that protruded from his reddish colored face. He was an extremely obese man who always had a cigarette hanging from his mouth and a scowl wrinkling his forehead.

The interesting thing about this man was the way he delivered the papers. He did not accomplish his route on foot, like some. He did not even pedal a bike like some of the other paperboys you see. He delivered papers in his car. The queerest thing about this was that his route was right in his own neighborhood! It included the two blocks that surrounded his house.

He began his work each day by pulling an old, rusty car out of his driveway. It was clear to everyone when he started because the muffler was so loud. He first pulled into his neighbors driveway and threw a paper out of his car window and onto their porch (or as close as he could come in one shot). He never once got out of the car when he missed the porch. Papers wound up on lawns, rooftops, and sidewalks. After he threw a paper from the window, he backed out of that driveway only to pull directly into the next. He reached out the window and threw another paper in the same fashion. He did this every afternoon for over an hour. It seemed to everyone that he could finish his route much quicker if he would walk.

You've got to be thinking by now, "Why?" Number one, "Why is a grown man delivering papers?" Two, "Why doesn't he walk, especially if the weather is nice? He could be enjoying the fresh air and beautiful outdoors." Or three, "Doesn't he realize the exercise might do him some good?" The day can be wonderfully sunny and warm, and there he sits trapped in a car filled with smoke, pulling in and out of driveways.

None of us can say exactly what motivates others to do what they do. But we are called to love everyone as God's children. Many fall prey to addiction and lose touch with their surroundings. Some suffer from emotional disorders such as depression and anxiety and cannot fully enjoy or appreciate life. Others simply have never experienced the awesome wonder and excitement, the true contentment and infinite satisfaction that comes from living in the heart of those dreams God places deep within the soul.

The man delivering papers might not even realize that something is not right in his life. He may be content riding in his old, rusty car and not having to walk. It may be he finds it difficult to exercise. Perhaps, he suffers from the complications of smoking such as chronic obstructive pulmonary disease or emphysema. Maybe he can sense a void and just doesn't care.

The beginning of this book shares the story about the woman who walked the same route every day. This unfinished story ends a thought provoking potpourri of the lessons God presents in life and His simple, yet gracious, miracles that challenge readers to explore their inner motivations. I believe that each person who has read this book has found themselves within one of its chapters. The turn of a page has turned the soul of every reader. We can all identify with at least one of the characters in this book. As diverse as we are, we all have one fundamental, yet precious bond with each other: Everyone's soul longs to become one with our Creator. Our hearts long to be complete. I sense that many more would chose to walk in the shoes of the woman in the first chapter of this book if given the choice to follow her path rather than that of the man delivering papers in his smoke filled car. The springtime wind filled the woman's spirit. Her soul swelled with the beauty of God's creation. Peace walked by her side. She was surrounded by a warm glow. Her home was born in the freedom she found in her soul, and her destination remained with her wherever she was.

The main problem is we do not always see our choices. Perception becomes distorted in today's world and we lose sight of what really matters, what really is, and that which will always be. Some of us fail to embrace our spiritual destinies. We do not always see, hear, or feel all of the blessings God presents, just waiting for us to unwrap as gifts each and every day.

None of the characters in this book are unique. They all have something in common…They are all children of God. Created with many gifts and talents, they go on to either make the most of their blessings or ignore them until it is too late. Thankfully, God highlights our days with miracles and lessons, big and small, which can be constant reminders to return to the path of light. Perhaps one of the most difficult challenges in life is staying attuned to the tiny treasures God places along our path. We cannot discover His gifts when the eyes of our souls are covered. His miracles never cease! Life is a constant display of God's omnipotence, if we simply participate in awe and grateful wonder.

Like the characters in this book, we all have choices. Life is not a passive parade of events; we can embrace our creation. We all have the innate ability to be the shining miracles that God intends us to be. We can choose to trust in God and have faith in His works. As we touch the hearts around us, we are touching heaven!

Choosing to recognize God's miracles and learn from the lessons He presents in life will help us stay on the narrow, yet glorious path that begins and ends in Jesus. Following God's will as each day unfolds places us one day closer to our eternal destiny. Staying in touch with our own soul opens a channel of power that will help us touch the soul of another.

Life's lessons demonstrated through God's miracles mold and shape us to become all that we are meant to be. Thank God He cares for us so much! No matter how many chances we have already spent, we are free to receive another opportunity. No matter how many times we turn away, His gentle grace waits patiently to embrace our spirit once again when we return to His path. I challenge everyone to step onto the path of faith and happiness! It is here that our souls will truly be made free.

Amy now conducts a one-day seminar which provides a God-centered 12-step approach to recovering from the pain we incur in life. The focus of the seminar is on building faith. It is an excellent workshop for churches and organizations to use to reach out to hurting members and also to the community at large.

For more information, write to:

Faith and Recovery Seminar
Attention: Amy Lynn
16785 255th Ave.
Spirit Lake, IA 51360

Or email to: amylynn@rconnect.com